TYRANT

ALSO BY STEPHEN GREENBLATT

The Rise and Fall of Adam and Eve

The Swerve: How the World Became Modern

Shakespeare's Freedom

Will in the World: How Shakespeare Became Shakespeare

Hamlet in Purgatory

Practicing New Historicism (with Catherine Gallagher)

Marvelous Possessions: The Wonder of the New World

Learning to Curse: Essays in Early Modern Culture

*Shakespearean Negotiations: The Circulation
of Social Energy in Renaissance England*

Renaissance Self-Fashioning: From More to Shakespeare

Sir Walter Ralegh: The Renaissance Man and His Roles

Three Modern Satirists: Waugh, Orwell, and Huxley

TYRANT

SHAKESPEARE ON POLITICS

STEPHEN
GREENBLATT

W. W. NORTON & COMPANY

Independent Publishers Since 1923

NEW YORK · LONDON

For information about permission to reproduce selections from this book,
write to Permissions, W. W. Norton & Company, Inc., 500 Fifth Avenue,
New York, NY 10110

For information about special discounts for bulk purchases, please contact
W. W. Norton Special Sales at specialsales@wwnorton.com or 800-233-4830

Manufacturing by LSC Communications, Harrisonburg
Book design by Marysarah Quinn
Production manager: Anna Oler

ISBN 978-0-393-63575-1

W. W. Norton & Company, Inc., 500 Fifth Avenue, New York, N.Y. 10110
www.wwnorton.com

W. W. Norton & Company Ltd., 15 Carlisle Street, London W1D 3BS

1 2 3 4 5 6 7 8 9 0

To Joseph Koerner and Luke Menand

CONTENTS

TYRANT

One

OBLIQUE ANGLES

FROM THE EARLY 1590S, at the beginning of his career, all the way through to its end, Shakespeare grappled again and again with a deeply unsettling question: how is it possible for a whole country to fall into the hands of a tyrant?

"A king rules over willing subjects," wrote the influential sixteenth-century Scottish scholar George Buchanan, "a tyrant over unwilling." The institutions of a free society are designed to ward off those who would govern, as Buchanan put it, "not for their country but for themselves, who take account not of the public interest but of their own pleasure."[1] Under what circumstances, Shakespeare asked himself, do such cherished institutions, seemingly deep-rooted and impregnable, suddenly prove fragile? Why do large numbers of people knowingly accept being lied to? How does a figure like Richard III or Macbeth ascend to the throne?

Such a disaster, Shakespeare suggested, could not happen without widespread complicity. His plays probe the psychological mechanisms that lead a nation to abandon its ideals and even its self-interest. Why would anyone, he asked himself, be drawn to a leader manifestly unsuited to govern, someone dangerously impulsive or viciously conniving or indifferent to the truth? Why, in some circumstances, does evidence of mendacity, crudeness, or cruelty serve not as a fatal disadvantage but as an allure, attracting ardent followers? Why do otherwise proud and self-respecting people submit to the sheer effrontery of the tyrant, his sense that he can get away with saying and doing anything he likes, his spectacular indecency?

Shakespeare repeatedly depicted the tragic cost of this submission—the moral corruption, the massive waste of treasure, the loss of life—and the desperate, painful, heroic measures required to return a damaged nation to some modicum of health. Is there, the plays ask, any way to stop the slide toward lawless and arbitrary rule before it is too late, any effective means to prevent the civil catastrophe that tyranny invariably provokes?

The playwright was not accusing England's current ruler, Elizabeth I, of being a tyrant. Quite apart from whatever Shakespeare privately thought, it would have been suicidal to float such a suggestion onstage. Dating back to 1534, during the reign of the queen's father, Henry VIII, legal statutes made it treason to refer to the ruler as a tyrant.[2] The penalty for such a crime was death.

There was no freedom of expression in Shakespeare's England, on the stage or anywhere else. The 1597 performances of an allegedly seditious play called *The Isle of Dogs* led to the arrest and imprisonment of the playwright Ben Jonson and to a government order—fortunately not enforced—to demolish all the playhouses in London.[3] Informants attended the theater, eager to claim a reward for denouncing to the authorities anything that could be construed as subversive. Attempts to reflect critically on contemporary events or on leading figures were particularly risky.

As with modern totalitarian regimes, people developed techniques for speaking in code, addressing at one or more removes what most mattered to them. But it was not only caution that motivated Shakespeare's penchant for displacement. He seems to have grasped that he thought more clearly about the issues that preoccupied his world when he confronted them not directly but from an oblique angle. His plays suggest that he could best acknowledge truth—to possess it fully and not perish of it—through the artifice of fiction or through historical distance. Hence the fascination he found in the legendary Roman leader Caius Martius Coriolanus or in the historical Julius Caesar; hence the appeal of such figures from the English and Scottish chronicles as York, Jack Cade, Lear, and, above all, the quintessential tyrants Richard III and Macbeth. And hence, too, the lure of entirely imaginary figures: the sadistic emperor Saturninus in *Titus Andronicus*; the corrupt deputy Angelo in *Measure for Measure*; the paranoid King Leontes in *The Winter's Tale*.

Shakespeare's popular success suggests that many of his contemporaries felt the same thing. Liberated from the surrounding circumstances and liberated, too, from the endlessly repeated clichés about patriotism and obedience, his writing could be ruthlessly honest. The playwright remained very much part of his place and time, but he was not their mere creature. Things that had been maddeningly unclear came into sharp focus, and he did not need to remain silent about what he perceived.

Shakespeare understood, as well, something that in our own time is revealed when a major event—the fall of the Soviet Union, the collapse of the housing market, a startling election result—manages to throw a garish light on an unnerving fact: even those at the center of the innermost circles of power very often have no idea what is about to happen. Notwithstanding their desks piled high with calculations and estimates, their costly network of spies, their armies of well-paid experts, they remain almost completely in the dark. Looking on from the margins, you dream that if you could only get close enough to this or that key figure, you would have access to the actual state of affairs and know what steps you need to take to protect yourself or your country. But the dream is a delusion.

At the beginning of one of his history plays, Shakespeare introduces the figure of Rumor, in a costume "painted full of tongues," whose task is ceaselessly to circulate stories "blown by surmises, jealousies, conjectures" (2 *Henry IV* Induction 16).[4] Its effects are painfully apparent in disastrously misinterpreted signals, fraudulent comforts, false alarms, sudden lurches from wild hope to suicidal despair. And the figures most deceived are not the gross multitude but, rather, the privileged and powerful.

For Shakespeare, then, it was easier to think clearly when the noise of those babbling tongues was silenced and easier to tell the truth at a strategic distance from the present moment. The oblique angle allowed him to lift off the false assumptions, the time-honored beliefs, and the misguided dreams of piety and to look unwaveringly at what lay beneath. Hence his interest in the world of classical antiquity, where Christian faith and monarchical rhetoric do not apply; his fascination with the pre-Christian Britain of *King Lear* or *Cymbeline*; his engagement with the violent eleventh-century Scotland of *Macbeth*. And even when he came closer to his own world, in the remarkable sequence of history plays extending from the fourteenth-century reign of Richard II to the downfall of Richard III, Shakespeare carefully kept at least a full century between himself and the events he depicted.

At the time he was writing, Elizabeth I had been queen for more than thirty years. Though she could on occasion be prickly, difficult, and imperious, her fundamental respect for the sanctity of the realm's political institutions was not generally in doubt. Even those who advocated a more aggressive foreign policy or clamored for a harsher crackdown on domestic subversion than she was willing to authorize ordinarily acknowledged her prudent sense of the limits to her power. Shakespeare is very unlikely to have regarded her, even in his most private thoughts, as a tyrant. But, like the rest of his countrymen, he had every reason to worry about what lay just ahead. In 1593, the queen celebrated her sixtieth birthday. Unmarried and childless, she stubbornly refused to name a successor. Did she think she was going to live forever?

For those with any imagination, there was more to worry about than the stealthy assault of time. It was widely feared that the kingdom faced an implacable enemy, a ruthless international conspiracy whose leaders trained and then dispatched abroad fanatical secret agents bent on unleashing terror. These agents believed that killing people labeled as misbelievers was no sin; on the contrary, they were doing God's work. In France, the Netherlands, and elsewhere they had already been responsible for assassinations, mob violence, and wholesale massacres. Their immediate goal in England was to kill the queen, crown in her place one of their sympathizers, and subjugate the country to their own twisted vision of piety. Their overarching goal was world domination.

The terrorists were not easy to identity, since most of them were home-grown. Having been radicalized, lured abroad to training camps, and then smuggled back into England, they blended easily into the mass of ordinary, loyal subjects. Those subjects were understandably reluctant to turn in their own kin, even ones suspected of harboring dangerous views. The extremists formed cells, praying in secret together, exchanging coded messages, and trolling for other likely recruits, drawn largely from the population of disaffected, unstable youths prone to dreams of violence and martyrdom. Some of them were in clandestine contact with the representatives of foreign governments who hinted darkly at invasion fleets and support for armed uprisings.

England's spy services were highly alert to the danger: they planted moles in the training camps, systematically opened correspondence, listened in on conversations in taverns and inns, and carefully scrutinized ports and border crossings. But the danger was difficult to eradicate, even when the authorities managed to get their hands on one or more of the suspected terrorists and questioned them under oath. After all, these were fanatics licensed by their religious leaders to deceive and instructed in what was called "equivocation," a method of misleading without technically lying.

If the suspects were interrogated under torture, as was routinely done, they were still often difficult to break. According to a report sent to the queen's spymaster, the extremist who assassinated Holland's Prince of Orange in 1584—the first man ever to kill a head of state with a handgun—remained uncannily obdurate:

> The same evening he was beaten with ropes and his flesh cut with split quills, after which he was put into a vessel of salt and water, and his throat was soaked in vinegar and brandy; and notwithstanding these torments, there was no sign whatever of distress or repentance, but, on the contrary, he said he had done an act acceptable to God.[5]

"An act acceptable to God": these were people brainwashed to believe that they would be rewarded in heaven for their acts of treachery and violence.

The menace in question, according to the zealous Protestants of late-sixteenth-century England, was Roman Catholicism. To the intense vexation of the queen's principal advisers, Elizabeth herself was reluctant to call the threat by its name and to take what they regarded as the necessary measures. She did not wish to provoke an expensive and bloody war with powerful Catholic states or to tar an entire religion with the crimes of a few fanatics. Unwilling, in the words of her spymaster Francis Walsingham, "to make windows into men's hearts and secret thoughts,"[6] for many years she allowed her subjects quietly to hold on to their Catholic beliefs, provided that they outwardly conformed to the official state religion. And, despite vehement urgings, she repeatedly refused to sanction the execution of her Catholic cousin Mary, Queen of Scots.

Having been driven out of Scotland, Mary was being held, without charge or trial, in a kind of protective detention in the north of England. Since she had a strong hereditary claim to the English throne—stronger, some thought, than Elizabeth herself—she was the obvious focus for the machinations of the Catholic powers of Europe and for the overheated daydreams and dangerous conspiracies of Catholic extremists at home. Mary herself was foolhardy enough to sanction sinister designs on her behalf.

The mastermind behind these designs, it was widely believed, was none other than the pope in Rome; his special forces were the Jesuits, sworn to obey him in everything; his hidden legions in England were the thousands of "Church papists" who dutifully attended Anglican services but harbored allegiance to Catholicism in their hearts. When Shakespeare was coming of age, rumors of the Jesuits—officially banned from entering the country, on pain of death—and the threats that they posed circulated widely. Their actual numbers may have been few, but the fear and loathing they aroused (along with clandestine admiration in some quarters) were considerable.

It is impossible to determine with any certainty where Shakespeare's innermost sympathies lay. But he cannot have been neutral or indifferent. Both of his parents had been born into a Catholic world, and for them, as for most of their contemporaries, the links to that world survived the Reformation. There was every reason for wariness and circumspection, and not merely because of the harsh punishments meted out by the Protestant authorities. The menace in England attributed to militant Catholicism was by no means entirely imaginary. In 1570, Pope Pius V issued a bull excommunicating Elizabeth as a heretic and a "servant of crime." The queen's subjects were released from any obligation they might have sworn to her; indeed, they were solemnly enjoined to disobey. A decade later, Pope Gregory XIII suggested that killing England's queen would not be a mortal sin. On the contrary, as the papal secretary of state declared on his master's behalf, "there is no doubt that whosoever sends her out of the world with the pious intention of doing God service, not only does not sin but gains merit."[7]

That declaration was incitement to murder. Though most

English Catholics wanted nothing to do with such violent measures, a few took it in their heads to try to rid the country of its heretical ruler. In 1583, the government's spy network discovered a conspiracy, with the collusion of the Spanish ambassador, to assassinate the queen. All through the years that followed there were comparable stories of dangers narrowly averted: letters intercepted, weapons seized, Catholic priests captured. Alerted by suspicious neighbors, officers would descend on rural safe houses, where they would smash cupboards, tap on walls for telltale hollow sounds, and rip up floorboards in search of so-called priests' holes. But still Elizabeth did nothing to eliminate the threat posed by Mary. "God open her Majesty's eyes," prayed Walsingham, "to see her peril."[8]

The queen's inner circle took the highly irregular step of drawing up a "Bond of Association," whose signers pledged to take revenge not only on anyone who made an attempt on the queen's life but also on any potential claimant to the throne—Mary was the obvious target—in whose interest such an attempt, successful or not, had been made. In 1586, Walsingham's spies got wind of another plot, this time involving a wealthy twenty-four-year-old Catholic gentleman named Anthony Babington, who, together with a group of like-minded friends, had persuaded himself that it was morally acceptable to kill the "tyrant." Using double agents who had penetrated the group and deciphered its secret codes, the authorities watched and waited as the conspiracy slowly unfolded. Indeed, when Babington began to get cold feet, one of Walsingham's agents provocateurs urged him on. The strategy paid the dividend the Protestant hard-liners had most hoped for: not only did the net catch fourteen conspirators, who were duly convicted of treason and then hanged, drawn, and quartered, but it also ensnared the careless, conniving Mary.

Like the killing of Osama bin Laden in 2011, the beheading of Mary on February 8, 1587, did not end the threat of terrorism in England; nor did it end with the defeat of the Spanish Armada the following year. If anything, the country's mood darkened. Another foreign invasion seemed imminent. The government's spies continued their work; Catholic priests continued to venture into England and minister to their increasingly desperate and beleaguered flock; wild rumors continued to circulate. A day laborer was forced to stand in the pillory in 1591 for having said, "We shall never have a merry world while the Queen liveth"; another received a similar punishment for declaring that "this is no good government which we now live under . . . and if the Queen die there will be a change and all those that be of this religion now used will be pulled out."[9] At Sir John Perrot's treason trial in 1592, it was reported as a serious charge that he had described the queen as "a base bastard piss-kitchen woman." In the Star Chamber, the Lord Keeper complained of all the "railing open speeches [and] false, lying, traitorous libels" circulating in London.[10]

Even if loose talk bordering on treason could somehow be shrugged off, there was still the succession issue to worry about. The queen's fluorescent red wig and her extravagant jeweled gowns could not conceal the passage of years. She had arthritis, her appetite failed her, and she began to use a staff to steady herself when she climbed stairs. She was, as her courtier Sir Walter Ralegh delicately put it, "a lady whom Time has surprised." Yet she would not name a successor.

Late Elizabethan England knew in its heart that the whole order of things was utterly fragile. The anxiety was by no means restricted only to a small Protestant elite eager to preserve its dominance. Beleaguered Catholics had argued for years that the queen was surrounded by Machiavellian politicians, each of whom was constantly maneuvering to advance the interests of his faction, stirring up paranoid fears of Catholic conspiracies, and waiting for the critical moment when he could seize tyrannical power for himself. Disgruntled Puritans had a comparable set of fears focused on a similar cast of characters. Anyone concerned about the country's religious settlement, about the distribution of wealth, about its foreign relations, about the possibility of civil war—that is, almost anyone who was fully sentient in the 1590s—must have brooded about the state of the queen's health and talked about rival favorites and counselors at court, the threat of Spanish invasion, the clandestine presence of Jesuits, the agitation of Puritans (then called Brownists), and other reasons for alarm.

Most of the talk, to be sure, had to be in whispers, but it went on all the time in the obsessive, round-and-round-the-same-track way that political discussions always go. Shake-

speare repeatedly depicts minor characters—the gardeners
in *Richard II*, nameless Londoners in *Richard III*, soldiers on
the eve of battle in *Henry V*, starving plebeians in *Coriolanus*,
cynical subalterns in *Antony and Cleopatra*, and the like—
sharing rumors and debating matters of state. Such reflections
by the lowly upon their betters tended to enrage the elite:
"Go, get you home, you fragments" (*Coriolanus* 1.1.214), an
aristocrat snarls at a group of protesters. But the fragments
could not be silenced.

None of England's national security concerns, major or
minor, could be depicted directly on the stage. The theater companies that thrived in London were feverishly in
search of exciting stories, and they would have loved to
draw audiences with the equivalent of television's *Homeland*. But the Elizabethan theater was censored, and though
on occasion the censor could be lax, he would never have
permitted the staging of plots that depicted threats to the
queen's regime, let alone allowed the public impersonation
of figures like Mary, Queen of Scots, Anthony Babington,
or Elizabeth herself.[11]

Censorship inevitably generates techniques of evasion.
Like Midas's wife, people feel compelled to talk, if only to
the wind and the reeds, about whatever is most deeply disturbing to them. Theater companies, competing fiercely with
one another, had a strong economic incentive for addressing this compulsion. They discovered that it was possible to
do so by shifting the scene to far-off places or by depicting
events in the distant past. On rare occasions, the censor found

the parallels too obvious or demanded proof that historical events were being correctly rendered, but for the most part he winked at the subterfuge. Perhaps the authorities recognized that some escape valve was necessary.

Shakespeare was the supreme master of displacement and strategic indirection. He never wrote what were called "city comedies," plays in contemporary English settings, and, with very rare exceptions, he kept a safe distance from current events. He was drawn to plots that unfolded in places like Ephesus, Tyre, Illyria, Sicily, Bohemia, or a mysterious, nameless island in a remote sea. When he engaged with fraught historical events—succession crises, corrupt elections, assassinations, the rise of tyrants—these happened in ancient Greece and Rome or in prehistoric Britain or in the England of his great-great-grandparents and earlier. He felt free to alter and reshape the materials he drew from the chronicle histories, in order to produce more compelling and pointed stories, but he worked with identifiable sources, which, if required by the authorities, he could cite in his defense. He was understandably reluctant to spend time in prison or have his nose slit.

There was only one notable exception to this lifelong strategy of indirection. *Henry V,* which Shakespeare wrote in 1599, depicts the spectacular military triumph, almost two centuries earlier, of an English army that had invaded France. Toward the end of the play, a chorus invites the audience to imagine the glorious reception the victorious king received when he returned to his capital: "Behold/In the quick forge and working-house of thought/How London doth pour out her citizens" (5.0.22–24). Then, on the heels of this image of a popular celebration in the nation's past, the chorus conjures up a comparable scene it hopes to witness in the near future:

> Were now the General of our gracious Empress,
> As in good time he may, from Ireland coming,
> Bringing rebellion broachèd on his sword,
> How many would the peaceful city quit
> To welcome him! (5.0.30–34)

The "General" in question was the queen's favorite, the Earl of Essex, who was at that moment leading English forces against Irish insurgents led by Hugh O'Neill, Earl of Tyrone.

It is not clear why Shakespeare decided to refer directly to a current event—and one that could only be hoped for "in good time."[12] Perhaps the playwright was urged to do so by his patron, the wealthy Earl of Southampton, to whom Shakespeare had dedicated his poems *Venus and Adonis* and *The Rape of Lucrece*. Essex's close friend and political ally, Southampton knew that his vainglorious, debt-ridden friend avidly courted popular acclaim, and the theater was the perfect venue for reaching the masses. Accordingly, he may have hinted to the playwright that a patriotic anticipation of the general's impending triumph would be most welcome. It would have been difficult for Shakespeare to have refused.

As it happened, shortly after *Henry V* was first performed, the headstrong Essex did indeed return to London, but not with the head of Hugh O'Neill spitted on his sword. Facing the abject failure of his military campaign, he had thrown up his hands and left Ireland, against the queen's explicit orders that he remain there. He decided to come home.

What then unfolded were a series of events that quickly built to a crisis at the very center of the regime. Essex's precipitous and unwelcome return—still mud-spattered, he burst in upon the queen, threw himself at her feet, and ranted wildly about those who hated him—gave his principal enemies at court—her chief minister, Robert Cecil, and her favorite, Walter Ralegh—the opportunity they long had sought. Outmaneuvered and increasingly agitated, the earl saw the queen's favor slipping away. Always hard-pressed to control himself, he made the fatal mistake of uttering in a rage that the queen had grown "old and cankered" and that her mind "was become as crooked as her carcass."[13]

Court culture inevitably generates fiercely competing factions, and Elizabeth had for years brilliantly played one off against another. But with her increasing debility, the old enmities sharpened and became murderous. When the Privy Council summoned Essex for a meeting on state business, he refused to go, declaring that he would be assassinated on Ralegh's orders. His tangle of fear and loathing, coupled with a delusional confidence that the populace of London would rise up to support him, ultimately led Essex to stage an armed rising against the queen's counselors and perhaps against the queen herself. The rising failed miserably. Essex and his principal allies, including the Earl of Southampton, were arrested.

Ralegh urged Cecil, who conducted the official inquiry, not to let slip the golden opportunity to destroy their hated enemy once and for all: if you "relent towards this tyrant," he wrote, "you will repent it when it shall be too late."[14] "Tyrant" here is something more than a random insult. If Essex were to recover his preeminence, Ralegh implies, he would be in a position, given the queen's advanced years, to rule the kingdom, and he would no doubt dispense with legal niceties. He would be eager to get rid of his rivals—and this would not mean politely asking them to retire. He would do what tyrants do.

After Cecil finished with his inquiry, Essex and South-ampton were put on trial, convicted of high treason, and sentenced to die. Southampton's sentence was commuted to life imprisonment, but for the queen's onetime favorite, there was no mercy. Essex was executed on February 25, 1601. The government saw to it that the abject confession he allegedly made on the scaffold—he had planned the treasonous rising, he said, and was now "justly spewed out of the realm"—was duly published after his death.

Shakespeare had been a fool to get anywhere close to these vicious struggles. The uncharacteristic contemporary reference to the "General" in *Henry V* does not seem to have provoked an official response, but it could easily have led to disaster. For on the afternoon of Saturday, February 7, 1601, the day before the attempted coup, a number of Essex's key supporters, including his steward, Sir Gelly Meyrick, had taken a boat across the Thames to go to the Globe Theatre. A few days earlier, Meyrick's close associates had requested from the theater's resident company, the Lord Chamberlain's Servants, a performance of an earlier Shakespeare play, a play about "the deposing and killing of King Richard the Second." The actors objected; *Richard II* was an old play, they said, and it was not likely to draw a large crowd. Their objection was overcome when they were offered forty shillings on top of their ordinary fee of £10 for a command performance.

But why were Gelly Meyrick and the others so eager to have *Richard II* performed? It was not the idle impulse of a moment; at a crucial juncture, when they knew the stakes were life and death, it cost them planning, time, and money. They did not leave a record of their reasoning, but they presumably remembered that Shakespeare's play depicted the downfall of a ruler and his cronies. "I wasted time, and now doth time waste me" (5.5.49), the doomed king laments, after his rapacious counselors ("the caterpillars of the commonwealth," as the usurper calls them) have met the fate that Essex hoped to visit upon Cecil and Ralegh.

In *Richard II* it is not only the king's counselors who are killed by the usurper; it is the king himself. The usurper Bolingbroke never declares directly that he intends to topple the reigning monarch, let alone murder him. Like Essex, while he rails against the corruption of the ruler's inner circle, he dwells principally upon the injustice done to him personally. But having contrived Richard's abdication and imprisonment, and having had himself crowned as King Henry IV, he moves with cunning vagueness—the vagueness that confers what politicians call "deniability"—to take the essential last step. Fittingly, Shakespeare does not represent this move directly. Instead, he simply shows someone pondering what he has heard the king say:

> EXTON: Didst thou not mark the King what words
>   he spake?
>   "Have I no friend will rid me of this living fear?"
>   Was it not so?
> SERVANT: Those were his very words.
> EXTON: "Have I no friend?" quoth he. He spake it
>   twice,
>   And urged it twice together, did he not?
> SERVANT: He did.
> EXTON: And speaking it, he wistly looked on me,
>   As who should say, "I would thou wert the man
>   That would divorce this terror from my heart,"
>   Meaning the King at Pomfret. Come, let's go.
>   I am the King's friend and will rid his foe. (5.4.1–11)

That is the whole scene. It is over in a moment, but it is enough to conjure up an entire ethos of power in operation. No formal legal procedure is initiated against the deposed king. Instead, all that is needed is a pregnant hint, carefully repeated, conjoined with looks directed intently ("wistly") toward someone likely to grasp the hint's meaning.

There are always people in a new regime who will do any-thing to win the ruler's favor. Exton, as Shakespeare depicts him, is a nobody; this is the first time we see or hear of him.

He will undertake to become "the King's friend." "Let's go" (5.4.10), he says to his henchmen, and Richard is promptly murdered. Predictably enough, when Exton eagerly comes for his reward—"Great King, within this coffin I present/Thy buried fear" (5.6.30–31)—the ruler repudiates him: "Though I did wish him dead,/I hate the murderer, love him murdered" (5.6.39–40). "Love him murdered": with this deliciously bitter irony the play reaches its end.

Gelly Meyrick and his fellow conspirators certainly did not need to consult Shakespeare's play as a blueprint for their own actions. They had to have grasped that the circumstances the playwright depicted did not line up neatly with their own; they would not, in any case, have wanted to tip their hand. And to a modern reader, the tragedy's exploration of the poignant inner life of the fallen monarch seems very far from a piece of propaganda designed to incite the crowd to rise up in rebellion.

Yet the key must lie in the crowd. Command performances were most often held in private venues, before select audiences, but the Lord Chamberlain's Servants were paid to revive *Richard II* and perform it at the large outdoor public theater, before spectators most of whom paid a penny to stand and watch the show. Essex had always courted and counted on the support of the London crowd, the mob that Shakespeare invited his audience to imagine hurrying to welcome their triumphant general returning from Ireland as the glorious Henry V had returned from France. It hadn't worked out that way, but with *Richard II*, the conspirators must have felt that there was a benefit to be gained from representing to a large public (and perhaps to themselves as well) a successful coup d'état. Perhaps they wanted, quite simply, to make what they intended imaginable.[15]

By statutes dating back to 1352, it was treasonable "to compass or imagine" the death of the king or queen or of the principal public officials.[16] The use of the ambiguous term "imagine" left the government wide latitude to decide whom to prosecute, and it would certainly appear that the performance of *Richard II* at the Globe was treading on very dangerous ground. After all, Shakespeare's play staged for a mass audience the spectacle of the toppling and murder of a crowned king, together with the summary execution of the king's principal advisers. Yet the events depicted occurred in England's past, and by a tacit agreement, such distance in time provided a certain immunity, so that actions that in a contemporary setting would instantly arouse the censor's furious wrath and that might lead to criminal prosecution could be represented without great risk to the playwright and his company.

Nonetheless, the performance arranged by Meyrick called into question the tacit agreement that what was shown on stage, provided it kept its distance from current events, was mere play and hence did not matter. Quite the contrary: the Essex conspirators evidently thought it was strategically useful to have Shakespeare's tragedy about England's medieval past dusted off and presented at the Globe.

It is impossible to know what went through Meyrick's

mind when he watched *Richard II* that afternoon, but we do know how at least one person at the time understood its meaning. Six months after Essex's execution, Queen Elizabeth gave a gracious audience to William Lambarde, whom she had recently appointed Keeper of the Rolls and Records in the Tower of London. The learned archivist began dutifully going through an inventory of the records, reign by reign, that he had prepared for the queen. When he reached the reign of Richard II, Elizabeth suddenly declared, "*I am Richard II; know ye not that?*"[17] If her tone betrayed a touch of exasperation, it may be because the antiquarian seemed to have his nose so exclusively in the past, while she, like everyone else, was reflecting on the dark parallels between the events in the fourteenth century and Essex's attempted coup. Thinking on his feet, Lambarde quickly grasped that the key point lay in "imagining" the ruler's death. "Such a wicked imagination," he told the queen, "was determined and attempted by a most unkind Gentleman, the most adorned creature that ever your Majesty made." "This tragedy," Elizabeth responded hyperbolically, "was played forty times in open streets and houses." It is the theater—Shakespeare's theater—that offered the key to understanding the crisis of the present.

Shakespeare's direct allusion in *Henry V* to the Earl of Essex drew attention to searching political reflections throughout his plays that were safer left in the shadows. The queen, who had frequently commanded court performances, chose not to punish the players, as she could easily have done, and what might have been a disaster for Shakespeare and his entire company was narrowly averted. The playwright never again ventured so close to contemporary politics.

IN THE WAKE of the coup attempt, the special staging of *Richard II* became a focus of the government's investigation. One of Shakespeare's associates was compelled to testify before the Privy Council and explain what the Lord Chamberlain's Servants thought they were doing. His answer—merely making a bit of extra money—was accepted. Sir Gelly Meyrick was not so fortunate. Convicted on charges of arranging the special performance, along with other actions in support of rebellion, he was hanged, drawn, and quartered.

Two

PARTY POLITICS

IN A VERY EARLY TRILOGY, possibly written in collaboration with other playwrights, Shakespeare followed the twisting path from politics-as-usual to tyranny. The parts of *King Henry VI* are now among his least-known plays, but they first made him famous, and they remain acutely perceptive about the ways in which a society becomes ripe for a despot.

The starting point is weakness at the center of the realm. King Henry VI is still an untried youth, having succeeded to the throne upon the untimely death of his father, and the state is being managed by a Lord Protector, his uncle Duke Humphrey. Though this manager is selflessly committed to public service, his power is severely constrained, and he is surrounded by an array of thuggish, self-serving nobles. When the nobles complain that their king is a mere child, the Protector cuts through the phony nostalgia. The truth is, he tells them, that you actually prefer a weak ruler "Whom like a schoolboy you may overawe" (*1 Henry VI* 1.1.36). The power vacuum at the center gives the rivals space to maneuver and to plot against one another. But there are consequences to such partisan feuding: nothing gets done for the common good and, as we soon see, the factions are hardening into mortal enemies.

In a garden adjoining the buildings that housed London's law schools, two powerful noblemen, the Duke of York and the Duke of Somerset, are wrangling over the interpretation of a point of law. They appeal to those witnessing their argument to adjudicate between them, but the bystanders prudently decline to weigh in. The play provides no details about the legal issue over which they are quarreling; perhaps Shakespeare thought that it was finally not very important. What mattered was their unwillingness to compromise, the belligerent certainty felt by each that his position, and his alone, was the only possible one. "The truth appears so naked on my side," declares York, "That any purblind eye may find it out." "And on my side," replies Somerset, it is "So clear, so shining, and so evident/That it will glimmer through a blind man's eye" (2.4.20–24). There is no acknowledgment of a gray area here, no recognition that it might be possible for reasonable people to disagree. Each thinks it must be mere perversity not to admit what is so undeniably "evident."

Finding themselves deadlocked, they lack even the slightest inclination to move toward reconciliation. Instead, what Shakespeare depicts is a move toward a conflict that extends beyond these two individuals and their dependents to a much larger field. "Let him that is a true-born gentleman," York proclaims, "From off this brier pluck a white rose with me."

"Let him that is no coward nor no flatterer/But dare maintain the party of the truth," Somerset counters, "Pluck a red rose from off this thorn with me" (2.4.27–33). It is no longer possible for the bystanders to remain neutral, as they had at first tried to do. They must choose.

The historical York and Somerset were powerful feudal lords with private armies and effective control over particular parts of the island. The play could have depicted them in a way that would remind us of the warlords of contemporary Afghanistan. But instead it invites us, in effect, to watch the invention of political parties and the transformation of aristocratic rivals into political enemies. Shakespeare does not envisage these exactly in our terms: there was nothing in the parliamentary system of his time that corresponded to the partisan organizational structures that subsequently developed in England and elsewhere. What he shows is nonetheless oddly familiar. The roses serve as party badges; they designate two opposed sides. With a weird immediacy, the legal argument (whatever it was) gives way to blind adherence to the white or the red.

It is possible to imagine that political parties, by virtue of being large conglomerations of diverse people, could deflect the hostility of their leaders and encourage compromise. But here the opposite happens: as soon as the distinct party affiliations emerge, everyone's anger level suddenly seems to shoot up. "Now, Somerset, where is your argument?" asks York, to which Somerset replies that his argument is in his scabbard, thinking of what "Shall dye your white rose in a bloody red." York is comparably enraged: "This pale and angry rose," he

says, "As cognizance of my blood-drinking hate,/Will I forever and my faction wear" (2.4.59–109).

At the beginning of the scene, when called upon to offer
his opinion on one side or another of the legal argument,
the Earl of Warwick holds back. He may know something
about dogs and hawks, he genially declares, but in such
highly technical matters—"these nice sharp quillets of the
law" (2.4.17)—he professes to be no wiser than a jackdaw, a
proverbially stupid bird. But by the scene's end, in the wake
of the formation of the parties, his restraint has vanished: he
has plucked the white rose and is eager for blood. "This brawl
today," he prophesies,

> Grown to this faction in the Temple Garden,
> Shall send between the red rose and the white
> A thousand souls to death and deadly night.
>   (2.4.124–28)

The obscure legal difference has not fundamentally
changed, no new occasion for dispute has arisen, and there
does not seem to be an underlying cause such as greed or
jealousy. But the party rage seems to have a life of its own.
Suddenly everyone seems to be boiling over with potentially
murderous aggression. It is as if, in the absence of the dominant figure of the king, the purely conventional and mean-
ingless emblems precipitate a rush of both group solidarity
and group loathing.

This loathing is an important part of what leads to a social breakdown and, eventually, to tyranny. It makes the voice, even the very thought, of the opponent almost unendurable. You are either with me or against me—and if you are not with me, I hate you and want to destroy you and all of your adherents. Each party naturally seeks power, but seeking power becomes itself the expression of rage: I crave the power to crush you. Rage generates insults, and insults generate outrageous actions, and outrageous actions, in turn, heighten the intensity of the rage. It all begins to spiral out of control.

Everything does not fall apart at once. There is still a social order in place. Though beleaguered, Duke Humphrey remains in charge. And meanwhile the child king, whom he is serving as protector, is growing into a young man able to perceive the dangerous problem created by the wrangling parties and willing to speak out: "Civil dissension," he declares, "is a viperous worm/That gnaws the bowels of the commonwealth" (3.1.72–73). His observation is obviously true, but, unfortunately, he sounds more like a sententious moralist than a king. Henry does not have whatever it would take—charisma, cunning, or ruthlessness—to quell the bitterly feuding factions.

The weakness at the center is a provocation. Contemptuously dismissing young Henry's "bookish rule" (2 *Henry VI* 1.1.256), York jockeys for position against his enemies. He begins secretly to contemplate seizing the crown for himself, and he senses that others must be having the same thought for themselves. In order to ascend to the throne, he will have to destroy any potential rivals. Meanwhile, earnestly trying to pacify his fractious nobles, Henry gets them to stage a ceremony of reconciliation. Their anger, he says, strikes him as "brainsick"; it makes no sense that they are fighting over "slight and frivolous" (*1 Henry VI* 4.1.111–12) causes and fiercely adhering to emblems like the roses. But he is too weak to produce anything more than an empty charade of cooperation in the struggle against the French.

Part of the problem is Henry's fundamental decency. He is unable to see that Margaret, the beautiful French noble-woman to whom he has been married in an attempt to shore up England's claim to its overseas territory, is a cynical politician who is having an affair with the arrogant Marquess of Suffolk. The innocent young king appeals to sweet reason-ableness and to core moral values to which he believes that all men and women will readily assent.

Though he has himself scarcely reached full adulthood, the king sees the intransigent factional leaders as little more than spoiled and selfish children whose feverish party struggles are a perverse distraction from the issues that actually matter.

His high-minded contempt for their squabbles is perfectly understandable, but it only makes matters worse. When there are key appointments to be made—for example, who should be named regent over the territories that the English still hold in France?—Henry declares his indifference: "For my part, noble lords, I care not which:/Or Somerset or York, all's one to me" (*2 Henry VI* 1.3.100–101). But such detachment only creates scope for intensified competition. It would have been better had he expressed a preference or had he possessed a clearer understanding of the danger brewing just beneath the surface of the institutions over which he presides.

The one steady bulwark against impending chaos is Duke Humphrey, the Lord Protector. But, all too predictably, a cabal of cynical operatives, in the church as well as the royal entourage, conspire to bring him down. Falsely accused of treason, he tries to alert the king. If his destruction marked the end of his enemies' plotting, he tells Henry, he would willingly give up his life. "But mine is made the prologue to their play," he warns, "For thousands more that yet suspect no peril/Will not conclude their plotted tragedy" (3.1.151–53).

Henry hears the warning, but he is unable to save his principal adviser and friend. The deceitful Suffolk tells Parliament that the upright protector is "full of deep deceit." The murderous Cardinal Beaufort falsely accuses him of devising "strange deaths for small offenses done" (3.1.57–59). The mercenary York charges him with corruption. Buckingham sneers that these are merely "petty faults" compared with the ones that will soon come to light. The adulterous queen, sly, sadistic Margaret, calls Duke Humphrey a "loser" (3.1.182). The king does not believe the accusations—"My conscience tells me you are innocent" (3.1.141)—but he is powerless to stop the traps that are being sprung one after another. When the protector is led off under guard to answer the charges, Henry leaves Parliament in despair, "With sad unhelpful tears, and with dimmed eyes" (3.1.218).

Duke Humphrey's enemies secretly hate one another, but they at least agree on one thing: they all want this single upright figure—"The map of honor, truth, and loyalty" (3.1.203), as Henry describes him—out of the way. Since they know that the charges they have brought against him are false and since they fear that the king's ardent support will make it difficult to engineer a conviction in the absence of real evidence, they determine to have him murdered. Though they are cynical and ruthless, they cannot openly admit, even in their vicious little circle, that it is to further their own private ends that they are aiming to eliminate the Lord Protector. Instead, they profess to be concerned for the good of the state and the welfare of the naïvely trusting king. Henry is "too full of foolish pity" (3.1.225), laments the wily queen; he is incapable of seeing through Duke Humphrey's wiles. To allow him to serve as Lord Protector, adds the rapacious York, is like asking a hungry eagle to protect a chicken. It is, sly Suffolk proposes, like making a fox the guardian of the flock. Just because this particular fox has not in fact done any harm does not alter the fact that he is a "crafty murderer." Therefore, "Before his chaps be stained with crimson blood" (3.1.254–60), he should be craftily destroyed.

These high-level political figures are playing a peculiar game. No one in the group believes for a moment that Duke Humphrey must be murdered in order to protect the king or save the state. Every word they speak is a lie, and each of the plotters is merely projecting his or her own predominant vice onto the intended victim. Since they are not in public, why don't they simply say what they mean?

There are several possible answers. First, they are all

politicians and, therefore, congenitally dishonest; the word "politician," for Shakespeare, was virtually synonymous with hypocrite. ("Get thee glass eyes," rages Lear. "And, like a scurvy politician,/Seem to see the things thou dost not" [*King Lear* 4.6.164–66]). Second, they distrust one another and do not know what may be reported outside the room in which they are speaking. Third, each harbors a secret hope that their lie and theirs alone will deceive the others. Fourth, pretending that they are virtuous, even when they know that they are not, makes them feel better about themselves. And fifth, they are all warily watching to see if anyone among them expresses even a slight reservation about the conspiracy, anything that would lead it to unravel. They want everyone to be on board.

When it is clear that there are no reservations, the worldly Cardinal Beaufort undertakes to make the necessary arrangements. "Say you consent and censure well the deed," he says, soliciting, one last time, everyone's assent, "And I'll provide his executioner." Then he adds the characteristically fraudulent note of loyal service: "I tender so the safety of my liege" (*2 Henry VI* 3.1.275–77). With everyone consenting, the cardinal does what he has promised: Duke Humphrey is quickly dispatched, strangled in his bed by the prelate's hired killers.

Notwithstanding all of their precautions, the conspirators do not succeed in hiding their crime. The scene was carefully staged to make it appear that the victim died of natural causes, but the state of the corpse suggests otherwise. "See," observes Warwick,

> his face is black and full of blood,
> His eyeballs further out than when he lived,
> Staring full ghastly like a strangled man;
> His hair upreared, his nostrils stretched with
>   struggling,
> His hands abroad displayed, as one that grasped
> And tugged for life and was by strength
>   subdued. . . .
> It cannot be but he was murdered here.
>   (3.2.168–77)

The king is devastated, and the common people, who always loved the upright Duke Humphrey, angrily demand that the likeliest perpetrators, Suffolk and Cardinal Beaufort, be punished. Despite the queen's entreaties, the king exiles Suffolk—he ends up being killed at sea by pirates—and the cardinal falls ill and dies, raving wildly about the man whose murder he ordered.

But the damage has been done, and the state is teetering. Although Suffolk and the cardinal did most of the talking, the quiet force behind the killing of the Lord Protector was the feverishly ambitious York: "My brain, more busy than the laboring spider,/Weaves tedious snares to trap mine enemies" (3.1.339–40). A descendent of King Edward III, York is at the very top of the status hierarchy and prides himself on his royal blood. But it is precisely this rank-obsessed man—he rehearses his pedigree in numbing detail—who, to advance his cause, introduces a new element into the political struggle between the red rose and the white.

Up to this point, midway through the *Henry VI* trilogy, there have been very few glimpses of those at the bottom. Politics has been almost entirely the affair of the elites, who maneuver against one another, while the anonymous masses of messengers, servants, soldiers, guards, artisans, and peasants remain in the shadows. Now, suddenly and unexpectedly, the cast of characters changes: York sees an opportunity to forge an alliance with the miserable, overlooked, and ignorant lower classes, and he seizes upon it. And we learn that the hitherto invisible and silent poor are seething with anger. Party warfare cynically makes use of class warfare. The goal is to create chaos, which will set the stage for the tyrant's seizure of power.

Three

FRAUDULENT
POPULISM

IN DEPICTING THE aspiring tyrant's strategy, Shake-speare carefully noted among the landed classes of his time the strong current of contempt for the masses and for democracy as a viable political possibility. Populism may look like an embrace of the have-nots, but in reality it is a form of cynical exploitation. The unscrupulous leader has no actual interest in bettering the lot of the poor. Surrounded from birth with great wealth, his tastes run to extravagant luxuries, and he finds nothing remotely appealing in the lives of underclasses. In fact, he despises them, hates the smell of their breath, fears that they carry diseases, and regards them as fickle, stupid, worthless, and expendable. But he sees that they can be made to further his ambitions.

It is not the well-meaning king, or the principled civil servant Duke Humphrey, who understands what is down there at the very bottom of the realm. It is York's genius, if that is the right word for something so base, to grasp the use he can make of the resentment that seethes among the poorest of the poor. "I will stir up in England some black storm," he broods to himself, a storm that will not cease to rage until the crown he plans to seize—"the golden circuit on my head"—shines like the sun and calms the fury. And he has, he reveals, found the perfect person to be his agent: "I have seduced a headstrong Kentishman,/John Cade" (*2 Henry VI* 3.1.349–57).

John (or Jack) Cade was an actual person—a lower-class rebel about whom few personal details are known—who led a bloody popular revolt that flared up against the English government in 1450 and was quickly and violently suppressed. To fashion his character, Shakespeare cobbled together materials he gathered from the historical chronicles (including the charge that Cade was secretly funded by York), combined them with the traces of other peasant uprisings, and added details drawn from his own vivid imagination.

The grand Richard Plantagenet, Duke of York, does not care in the slightest about the ultimate fate of the base man he has seduced into furthering his designs, and he cares still less about the ragged mob he intends to stir up into rebellion. But he has observed Cade carefully and seen qualities that may make him useful, including an uncanny indifference to pain and, therefore, an ability to keep hidden their secret bond:

Say he be taken, racked, and tortured,
I know no pain they can inflict upon him
Will make him say I moved him to those arms.
   (3.1.376–78)

Secrecy is important: it would not do for the powerful aristocrat to be revealed as the instigator of a vicious popular uprising.

The uprising turns out to be an even greater storm than York could have wished. The mob, gathering just outside London in Blackheath, is rallied by Cade, who proves himself to be an effective demagogue, the master of voodoo economics:

There shall be in England seven halfpenny loaves
sold for a penny, the three-hooped pot shall have ten
hoops, and I will make it felony to drink small beer.
All the realm shall be in common. . . . [T]here shall
be no money; all shall eat and drink on my score.
   (4.2.61–68)

When the crowd roars its approval, Cade sounds exactly like a modern stump speaker: "I thank you, good people" (4.2.167).

The absurdity of these campaign promises is not an impediment to their effectiveness. On the contrary: Cade keeps producing demonstrable falsehoods about his origins and making wild claims about the great things he will do, and the crowds eagerly swallow them. To be sure, his neighbors know that Cade is a congenital liar:

> CADE: My mother a Plantagenet—
> BUTCHER: [*Aside*] I knew her well; she was a midwife.
> CADE: My wife descended of the Lacys—
> BUTCHER: [*Aside*] She was indeed a peddler's daughter and sold laces. (4.2.39–43)

Cade's absurd assertions of aristocratic lineage should make him seem merely a buffoon. Far from a wealthy, high-born magnate, he is little more than a vagabond: "I have seen him whipped three market days together" (4.2.53–54), whispers one of his supporters. But, strangely enough, this knowledge does not diminish the mob's faith.

Cade himself, for all we know, may think that what he is so obviously making up as he goes along will actually come to pass. Drawing on an indifference to the truth, shamelessness, and hyperinflated self-confidence, the loudmouthed demagogue is entering a fantasyland—"When I am king, as king I will be"—and he invites his listeners to enter the same magical space with him. In that space, two and two do not have to equal four, and the most recent assertion need not remember the contradictory assertion that was made a few seconds earlier.

In ordinary times, when a public figure is caught in a lie or simply reveals blatant ignorance of the truth, his standing is diminished. But these are not ordinary times. If a dispassionate bystander were to point out all of Cade's grotesque distortions, mistakes, and downright lies, the crowd's anger would light on the skeptic and not on Cade. Famously, it is at the end of one of Cade's speeches that someone in the crowd shouts, "The first thing we do, let's kill all the lawyers" (4.2.71).

Shakespeare knew that the line would get laughs, as it has done for the last four centuries. It releases the current of aggression that swirls around the whole enterprise of the law—directed not merely at venal attorneys but at all the agents of the vast social apparatus that compels the honoring of contracts, the payment of debts, the fulfillment of obligations. We blithely imagine that the crowd wants such responsible qualities in its leaders, but the scene suggests otherwise. What it wants instead is permission to ignore commitments, to violate promises, and to break the rules.

Cade begins by talking vaguely about "reformation," but his actual appeal is wholesale destruction. He urges the mob to pull down London's law schools, the Inns of Court, but that is only the beginning. "I have a suit unto your lordship," entreats one of his chief followers, "that the laws of England may come out of your mouth" (4.7.3–7). "I have thought upon it," Cade replies, "it shall be so. Away! Burn all the records of the realm; my mouth shall be the Parliament of England" (4.7.11–13).

That in this destruction the common people would lose even the very limited power they possess—the power expressed when they voted in parliamentary elections—does not matter. For Cade's ardent supporters, the time-honored institutional system of representation is worthless. It has, they feel, never represented *them*. Their inchoate wish is to tear up all the agreements, cancel all the debts, and wreck all the existing institutions. Better to have the law come from the mouth of the dictator, who may claim to be a Plantagenet but whom they recognize as one of their own. The masses are perfectly aware that he is a liar, but—venal, cruel, and self-serving though he is—he succeeds in articulating their dream: "Henceforward all things shall be in common" (4.7.16).

Cade's rant stands in for any transparency about his own past and any serious commitment to make good on this or that particular promise. Far from demanding that he keep his word, his followers are gratified when he rails against all contracts: "Is not this a lamentable thing, that the skin of an innocent lamb should be made parchment; that parchment, being scribbled o'er, should undo a man?" (4.2.72–75). The remark about the "scribbled-over" parchment is at once ridiculous—how else should legal documents look?—and canny. The poor whose passions Cade is arousing feel excluded, despised, and vaguely ashamed. They have been left out of an economy that increasingly demands possession of a once-esoteric technology: literacy. They do not imagine that they can master this new skill, nor does their leader propose that they undertake any education. It would hardly suit his purposes if they did so. What he does instead is manipulate their resentment of the educated.

The mob quickly apprehends a clerk and levels an accusation against him: "he can write and read." Indeed, his accusers report, "We took him setting of boys' copies" (4.2.81)—that is, preparing writing exercises for schoolboys. Cade undertakes to conduct the interrogation: "Dost thou use to write thy name," he asks. "Or hast thou a mark to thyself, like a honest plain-dealing man?" (4.2.92–93). If the clerk knew what was good for him, he would insist that he was illiterate and signed his name only with a mark. Instead he proudly proclaims his accomplishment: "Sir, I thank God I have been so well brought up that I can write my name." "He hath confessed!" the mob shouts. "Away with him! He's a villain and a traitor." "Away with him, I say!" orders Cade, echoing the crowd's demand. "Hang him with his pen and ink-horn about his neck" (4.2.94–99).

Jack Cade longs for the time when, as he puts it, boys played games of toss "for French crowns," a time before the country was "maimed and fain to go with a staff" (4.2.145–50). Until weaklings led it astray, he suggests, England compelled its enemies to tremble before its power, and that glorious swaggering must now be recovered. He promises to make England great again. How will he do that? He shows the crowd at once: he attacks education. The educated elite has betrayed the people. They are traitors who will all be brought to justice, and this justice will be meted out not by judges and lawyers but in a call-and-response between the leader and his mob. The English treasurer Lord Saye "can speak French"—"and therefore he is a traitor" (4.2.153). It makes perfect sense: "The Frenchmen are our enemies. . . . I ask but this: can he that speaks with the tongue of an enemy be a good counselor, or no?" The crowd roars the answer: "No, no—and therefore we'll have his head!" (4.2.155–58).

When the mob, having broken through London's defenses, streams into the city and captures this very Lord Saye, Cade experiences the full flush of triumph. He has in his hands the realm's highest fiscal officer, the emblem of the swamp that he has pledged to drain. (The demagogue's actual metaphor for what he intends to do is slightly homelier: "Be it known," he declares, "that I am the besom"—the broom—"that must sweep the court clean of such filth as thou art" [4.7.27–28].) With his excited followers hanging on every word, he enumerates the charges against his prisoner. He accuses Lord Saye of having done something even worse than giving up Normandy to the French:

> Thou hast most traitorously corrupted the youth of
> the realm in erecting a grammar school; and whereas,
> before, our forefathers had no other books but the
> score and the tally, thou hast caused printing to be
> used, and, contrary to the King, his crown, and dig-
> nity, thou hast built a paper mill. (4.7.28–33)

Helping foster an educated citizenry—people who read books—is Saye's most egregious crime. And Cade has corroborating evidence: "It will be proved to thy face that thou hast men about thee that usually talk of a noun and a verb and such abominable words no Christian ear can endure to hear" (4.7.33–36).

We are meant to find this ridiculous, of course; the scene is quite rightly played for laughs. But Shakespeare grasped something critically important: although the absurdity of the demagogue's rhetoric was blatantly obvious, the laughter it elicited did not for a minute diminish its menace. Cade and his followers will not slink away because the traditional political elite and the entirety of the educated populace regard him as a jackass.

That Cade himself understands the base of his power is suggested by the lines that immediately follow his drivel about nouns and verbs. "Thou hast appointed justices of the peace," he charges Lord Saye,

> to call poor men before them about matters they
> were not able to answer. Moreover, thou hast put
> them in prison and, because they could not read,
> thou hast hanged them, when indeed only for that
> cause they have been most worthy to live. (4.7.36–41)

In some sense, this rant is an extension of the rubbish Cade has been spouting: it is ridiculous for him to suggest that criminals deserve to be pardoned simply because they are illiterate. But the joke begins to curdle. The play has already amply shown that the rich and well-born can get away with murder. Moreover, Shakespeare's audience was well aware that the courts in their own time allowed something called "benefit of clergy," a legal device whereby those condemned to be executed for murder or theft could, if they demonstrated that they were literate, be remanded to jurisdictions which had no death penalty. Cade's accusation that those who could not read were hanged is perfectly accurate—and it gets at a whole legal system heavily weighted to favor the educated elite.

Small wonder then that there is a fathomless pool of lower-class resentment upon which Cade can draw, and small wonder, too, that the ridicule and contempt heaped upon him and his followers only intensifies this resentment. "Rebellious hinds, the filth and scum of Kent,/Marked for the gallows," the royal officer Sir Humphrey Stafford rails at the mob, "lay your weapons down!/Home to your cottages" (4.2.111–13). Calling them "filth and scum" simply helps highlight the ceremonious show of respect their leader offers them: "It is to you, good people, that I speak," Cade tells them, "Over whom, in time to come, I hope to reign,/For I am rightful heir unto the crown" (4.2.118–20). Once again he advances his grotesque lie, and once again there is an official attempt to expose it: "Villain, thy father was a plasterer," Stafford fumes. To this Cade replies, "And Adam was a gardener" (4.2.121–23).

This reply is something more than a simple non sequitur. Cade's words allude to the slogan of the Peasants' Revolt in the late fourteenth century: "When Adam delved and Eve span, who was then the gentleman?" The peasants' leader, the revolutionary priest John Ball, spelled out the meaning of his incendiary little rhyme: "From the beginning all men were created equal by nature." Before it was over, rebels had torched court records, opened jails, and killed officials of the crown.

Shakespeare carries over into his depiction of Cade's uprising the fear and loathing aroused among the propertied classes by lower-class insurgency. The peasant rebels are fueled by something like the murderous vision of Cambodia's Pol Pot: their goal is to destroy not merely the high-ranking nobles but the entire educated population of the country. "All scholars, lawyers, courtiers, gentlemen," one appalled observer reports. "They call false caterpillars and intend their death" (4.4.35–36). The common people have been exploited and enslaved; this is the moment for them to seize liberty. "We will not leave one lord, one gentleman," Cade chillingly promises, exhorting his followers to "Spare none but such as go in clouted shoon" (4.2.169–70)—that is, in the hobnailed boots of peasants. The rural poor have not joined the rebelling urban masses, but the peasants, as Cade puts it, are "such/ As would, but that they dare not, take our parts" (4.2.172). They are fellow travelers in the war of the ignorant against the literate and would, if they had the courage, applaud the grisly end he orders for the likes of the well-spoken Lord Saye: "Go, take him away, I say, and strike off his head presently, and then break into his son-in-law's house, Sir James Cromer, and strike off his head, and bring them both upon two poles hither" (4.7.99–101).

When his command is carried out, and the heads are duly brought to him, Cade arranges a piece of sadistic political theater. "Let them kiss one another," he orders, "for they loved well when they were alive." Then he adds, with the cruel sarcasm that perfectly typifies this kind of demagogue, "Now part them again, lest they consult about the giving up of some more towns in France" (4.7.119–22).

Cade aspires to being a tyrant, and a rich one at that: "The proudest peer in the realm shall not wear a head on his shoulders unless he pay me tribute" (4.7.109–10). He imagines for himself, as well, the right to sleep with all the women he can put his hands on. For a time, he manages to whip his followers into a frenzy of destructiveness: "Up Fish Street! Down Saint Magnus' Corner! Kill and knock down! Throw them into Thames!" (4.8.1–2). But he has no organizational skills or party on which to draw, and we know (though his followers do not) that he is merely the tool of the sinister York.

When the moment is ripe, by borrowing from Cade's own book and appealing to nativist sentiments and dreams of plunder, the royal authorities lure the mob away from their rebellion and in a different direction—"To France, to France, and get what you have lost!" Isolated and embittered, Cade flees for his life, cursing those who had followed him:

> I thought ye would never have given out these arms
> till you had recovered your ancient freedom. But you
> are all recreants and dastards and delight to live in
> slavery to the nobility. Let them break your backs with
> burdens, take your houses over your heads, ravish your
> wives and daughters before your faces. (4.8.23–29)

When we next see Cade, he is a starving fugitive, break-ing into a garden "to see if I can eat grass, or pick a salad" (4.10.6–7). The garden's owner easily dispatches the emaci-ated rebel with his sword and drags his corpse "Unto a dung-hill which shall be thy grave" (4.10.76).

King Henry breathes a sigh of relief, but the news of Cade's downfall is accompanied at almost the same moment by word that York, with an Irish army, is advancing toward the royal encampment. York is clever enough to keep his intentions hidden until he has strength enough to act, but he makes clear in his soliloquies that he will settle for nothing less than the crown. What follows is a complex tangle of events, mingling wars in France with domestic conspiracy, treachery, and violence. The outcome is full-scale war between the two parties, the red roses and the white, Lancastrians and Yorkists.

The horrors of this war epitomize the breakdown of basic values—respect for order, civility, and human decency—which paves the way for the tyrant's rise. The seeds of the breakdown had already been glimpsed in the argument between York and Somerset, where a disagreement over an obscure point of law had quickly escalated into a barrage of insults. The anger was intensified by the rise of party politics and then, through York's subterfuge, had led to the murder of Duke Humphrey and Jack Cade's rebellion. But civil war lifts the veil of subterfuge: the principal political figures no longer hide their highest ambitions or leave the enactment of their sadistic impulses to their subordinates. The byzan-tine complexity of the plot from this point forward has made the final play of Shakespeare's trilogy notoriously difficult to stage, but several things are particularly notable.

First, rising chaos makes the outcome of the struggle for power completely unpredictable. When he was operating in the half-shadows and effecting his wishes through substitutes like Cade, York had seemed almost invulnerable. But once he is in the open—at one point he actually seats himself on the throne, though he is quickly forced to step down—he and his family become direct targets of the opposing faction. His enemies capture and kill his twelve-year-old son. When, shortly afterward, they capture York himself, they mockingly offer him a handkerchief soaked in his son's blood. Then they taunt him and adorn him with a paper crown before stabbing him to death. Such is the vicious cruelty that he himself has helped to release and legitimate, and such, too, is the end of the would-be tyrant.

Second, the dream of absolute rule is not the goal of a single person alone; in the political conception of the age, it is a dynastic ambition, a family affair. In an age in which power routinely passed from father to the eldest son (or, in the absence of sons, to the eldest daughter), it made perfect sense for tyrants to model themselves after the monarchs they sought to displace and to attempt to secure power for their heirs. Even in democratic systems where succession is determined by vote, we have by no means left dynastic ambition behind; it seems, if anything, to be intensifying in contemporary politics. Besides, who can the perennially insecure tyrant trust more than the members of his own family?

But family interest is only one element in the continuing turmoil Shakespeare depicts. The turmoil is also a consequence of party politics, symbolized here by the plucking of the white and red roses. York's death is a significant blow to his party, but it by no means puts an end to the struggle to destroy the legitimate monarch. The Yorkists find a new candidate, York's son Edward, and advance his claim in any way they can.

Third, the political party determined to seize power at any cost makes secret contact with the country's traditional enemy. England's enmity with the nation across the Channel—constantly fanned by all the overheated patriotic talk of recovering its territories there, and fueled by all the treasure and blood spilled in the attempt to do so—suddenly vanishes. The Yorkists—who, in the person of Cade, had pretended to consider it an act of treason even to speak French— enter into a set of secret negotiations with France. Nominally, the negotiations aim to end hostilities between the two countries by arranging a dynastic marriage, but they actually spring, as Queen Margaret cynically observes, "from deceit, bred by necessity" (*3 Henry VI* 3.3.68). To bring Edward Plantagenet to the throne, the Yorkists seek to enhance their candidate's power. He still lacks the strength to topple Henry, and his party will obtain that strength wherever they can find it, even if it means betraying their country. It does not matter that the Yorkists have constantly lamented the loss of so much territory to their hated rivals, the French, and have vociferously blamed Henry for the loss. Now suddenly the Yorkists

make a show of "kindness and unfeigned love" (3.3.51) to
their enemy. Ardent patriots like Talbot are hopelessly naïve
to believe that loyalty to the nation trumps personal interest.
A cynical insider like Queen Margaret knows better: "How
can tyrants safely govern home," she asks, "Unless abroad
they purchase great alliance?" (3.3.69–70).

Fourth, the legitimate, moderate leader cannot count on
popular gratitude or support. In the chaotic free-for-all into
which the realm has fallen, this apparent betrayal of principle
does not produce any great outrage. What might at another
time have provoked charges of treason is simply accepted as
the way things are. And if there are no longer the expected
punishments for treachery, so, too, there are no longer the
anticipated rewards for virtue. Perhaps such anticipation was
always a delusion: a decent ruler should never count on the
gratitude of the people. That had already been demonstrated
in the Cade rebellion, but it is brought home again, still more
fatally, at the climax of the civil war. Just before his downfall, Henry expresses confidence that his subjects will support
him because he has always been a reasonably just, caring,
and moderate king. The claim is true enough; the mistake,
a fatal one, is to think that this will earn him secure popular
support. "I have not stopped mine ears to their demands,"
Henry reassures himself,

> Nor posted off their suits with slow delays.
> My pity hath been balm to heal their wounds;
> My mildness hath allayed their swelling griefs;

My mercy dried their water-flowing tears.
I have not been desirous of their wealth
Nor much oppressed them with great subsidies,
Nor forward of revenge, though they much erred.
Then why should they love Edward more than me?
  (4.9.7–15)

But when the moment of truth comes, in the battle that decides whether the Yorkists will finally succeed in seizing power, there is no rush of popular support for the virtuous Henry. First his son and heir is captured and stabbed to death by the sons of York, and then it is his own turn to die at the hands of Richard, Duke of Gloucester, the most ruthless of these sons. The Yorkist leader, Edward Plantagenet, ascends the throne.

And fifth, the apparent restoration of order, in the wake of national turmoil, may be an illusion. Eager to "spend the time/With stately triumphs, mirthful comic shows" (5.7.42–43), Edward is a more moderate figure than York, his father, far less consumed with fantasies of absolute power. To return the country to a semblance of normal, legitimate rule, he hopes to bring about a collective forgetting of the nightmare from which everyone has barely awakened. In this spirit of amnesia, he characterizes the bloodshed that his party has caused a "sour annoy." And he cheerfully declares that the threats have all vanished: "Thus have we swept suspicion from our seat/And made our footstool of security" (5.7.13–14).

Everything in the realm, in the new king's final words,

seems happily settled: "For here I hope begins our lasting joy" (5.7.46). Yet at the close of Shakespeare's Wars of the Roses trilogy, the audience knows that the joy will be anything but lasting. Edward largely owed his party's victory and, hence, his kingship to his stalwart brothers, George, Duke of Clarence, and Richard, Duke of Gloucester. George, to be sure, wavered at one point in the civil war, siding briefly with the Lancastrians, but he came back to fight for the Yorkist cause. Richard never wavered, and it was he who murdered Henry VI. But with the king bleeding to death at his feet, Richard had quietly made it clear that his only allegiance was to himself. "I have no brother," he declared. "I am myself alone" (5.6.80–83). A new tyrant is waiting in the wings.

Four

A MATTER
OF CHARACTER

SHAKESPEARE'S *RICHARD III* brilliantly develops the personality features of the aspiring tyrant already sketched in the *Henry VI* trilogy: the limitless self-regard, the law-breaking, the pleasure in inflicting pain, the compulsive desire to dominate. He is pathologically narcissistic and supremely arrogant. He has a grotesque sense of entitlement, never doubting that he can do whatever he chooses. He loves to bark orders and to watch underlings scurry to carry them out. He expects absolute loyalty, but he is incapable of gratitude. The feelings of others mean nothing to him. He has no natural grace, no sense of shared humanity, no decency.

He is not merely indifferent to the law; he hates it and takes pleasure in breaking it. He hates it because it gets in his way and because it stands for a notion of the public good that he holds in contempt. He divides the world into winners and losers. The winners arouse his regard insofar as he can use them for his own ends; the losers arouse only his scorn. The public good is something only losers like to talk about. What he likes to talk about is winning.

He has always had wealth; he was born into it and makes ample use of it. But though he enjoys having what money can get him, it is not what most excites him. What excites him is the joy of domination. He is a bully. Easily enraged, he strikes out at anyone who stands in his way. He enjoys seeing others cringe, tremble, or wince with pain. He is gifted at detecting weakness and deft at mockery and insult. These skills attract followers who are drawn to the same cruel delight, even if they cannot have it to his unmatched degree. Though they know that he is dangerous, the followers help him advance to his goal, which is the possession of supreme power.

His possession of power includes the domination of women, but he despises them far more than desires them. Sexual conquest excites him, but only for the endlessly reiterated proof that he can have anything he likes. He knows that those he grabs hate him. For that matter, once he has succeeded in seizing the control that so attracts him, in politics as in sex, he knows that virtually everyone hates him. At first that knowledge energizes him, making him feverishly alert to rivals and conspiracies. But it soon begins to eat away at him and exhaust him.

Sooner or later, he is brought down. He dies unloved and unlamented. He leaves behind only wreckage. It would have been better had Richard III never been born.

SHAKESPEARE BASED HIS portrait of Richard on a highly tendentious, partisan account written by Thomas More and reiterated by the Tudor chroniclers. But where, the playwright wondered, did his psychopathology come from? How was it formed? The tyrant, as Shakespeare conceived him, was inwardly tormented by a sense of his own ugliness, the consequence of a misshapen body that from the moment he was born made people recoil in disgust or horror. "The midwife wondered, and the women cried/'O Jesus bless us, he is born with teeth!'" (*3 Henry VI* 5.6.74–75). "And so I was," he reflects, "which plainly signified/That I should snarl and bite and play the dog."

Richard's neonatal teeth are a symbolically charged feature that he has incorporated into his account of himself and that has evidently been elaborated by others. "They say my uncle grew so fast," his little nephew York prattles, "That he could gnaw a crust at two hours old" (*Richard III* 2.4.27–28). "Who told thee so?" asks his grandmother, the Duchess of York, who is Richard's mother. "His nurse," the boy replies, but the duchess contradicts him: "His nurse? Why she was dead ere thou wert born" (2.4.33). "If 'twere not she," he says, "I cannot tell who told me" (2.4.34). Richard's infancy has become the stuff of legend.

Richard mentions the reaction of the midwife and the attending women, but it is easy to surmise that the account of his ill-omened arrival derives principally from his mother. The Duchess of York has evidently regaled her son and everyone else with stories of his difficult birth and the repellent signs on his body. Her recurrent theme is what she calls the "anguish, pain, and agony" (*Richard III* [Quarto] 4.4.156) she experienced in bringing him into the world, and that theme serves as a reproach leveled against him by those imprudent or desperate enough to speak their minds. "Thy mother felt more than a mother's pain," the unfortunate Henry VI reminds his captor Richard, "And yet brought forth less than a mother's hope—/To wit, an undigested and deformèd lump" (*3 Henry VI* 5.7.49–51). When the captive king goes on to bring up those teeth—"Teeth thou had in thy head when thou wast born/To signify thou cam'st to bite the world"—Richard has had enough. Shouting "I'll hear no more!" he stabs his royal prisoner to death (5.7.53–57).

As those around him come to perceive, something is seriously wrong with Richard's mind; even he acknowledges his inner turmoil, if only to himself. To account for his moral and psychological deformity, his contemporaries point to his physical deformity: the twisted spine they call a hunchback (and we would diagnose as severe kyphosis). For them, it is as if the universe marked him outwardly to signify his inner condition. And Richard concurs: "Then, since the heavens have shaped my body so," he says, "Let hell make crooked my mind to answer it" (5.6.78–79). Feeling in himself none of the ordinary human emotions—I have, he says, "neither pity, love, nor fear" (5.6.68)—he actively wills his mind to match the stigmatized crookedness of his body.

Shakespeare does not repudiate his culture's belief that

bodily deformity signified moral deformity; he allows his audience to credit the notion that a higher power, whether nature or God, has provided a visible sign of the villain's wickedness. Richard's physical deformity is a kind of preternatural portent or emblem of his viciousness. But, against the dominant current of his culture, Shakespeare insists that the inverse is also true: Richard's deformity—or, rather, his society's reaction to his deformity—is the root condition of his psychopathology. There is nothing automatic in this conditioning; certainly, no suggestion that all people with twisted spines become cunning murderers. Shakespeare does, however, suggest that a child unloved by his mother, ridiculed by his peers, and forced to regard himself as a monster will develop certain compensatory psychological strategies, some of them both destructive and self-destructive.

Richard observes his brother Edward wooing an attractive woman. It is evidently something he has watched before— his brother is a notorious ladies' man—and it arouses bitter reflections. "Love forswore me in my mother's womb," he broods, and to make sure that this abandonment would be permanent, the goddess connived with Nature

> To shrink mine arm up like a withered shrub,
> To make an envious mountain on my back,
> Where sits deformity to mock my body;
> To shape my legs of an unequal size,
> To disproportion me in every part.
>   (*3 Henry VI* 3.2.153–60)

It would be grotesque for him, he thinks, to imagine that he could have any erotic success; no one could ever love that body of his. Whatever pleasure he could seize from life thus could not possibly come from making his "heaven in a lady's lap" (3.2.148). But there is a way he can compensate for the painful loss: he can devote himself to bullying those who possess the natural endowments he lacks.

The youngest son of the Duke of York and the brother to the reigning king, Edward IV, Richard is near the top of the social hierarchy. He knows that people make cruel jokes about him when he is not in earshot, calling him the "toad" and the "boar," but he knows, too, that his high birth confers upon him almost limitless authority over those beneath him. To this authority he conjoins arrogance, a penchant for violence, and a sense of aristocratic impunity. When he gives an order, he expects it to be instantly obeyed. Encountering the procession bearing the hearse of the king he has killed, Richard peremptorily commands the gentlemen bearers and their armed attendants to stop and set it down. When they at first refuse, he showers insults upon them—"villains," "unmannered dog," "beggar"—and threatens to kill them (*Richard III* 1.2.36–42). Such is the force of his social position and the confidence with which he wields it that they tremble before him and obey.

Dominating others serves to shore up lonely Richard's damaged self-image, to ward off the pain of rejection, to keep him upright. It is for him as if his body were constantly mocking itself, as well as being mocked by others. Physically unbalanced, his body, he says, is "like to a chaos" (*3 Henry VI*

3.2.161). Exercising power, particularly the kind of power that throws people off balance, reduces his own sense of chaotic disproportionateness, or so at least he hopes. It is not simply a matter of commanding people to do what he wants them to do, though that is agreeable; it is also peculiar pleasure of making them tremble or totter or fall.

As Shakespeare's play depicts him, Richard is chillingly clear about the links that bind together his physical deformity, his psychological disposition, and his overarching political goal:

> since this earth affords no joy to me
> But to command, to check, to o'erbear such
> As are of better person [i.e., appearance] than myself,
> I'll make my heaven to dream upon the crown.
> (3.2.165–68)

In his own nasty way, he is a man who has achieved an unusual clarity about himself. He knows what he feels, what he lacks, and what he needs to have (or at least longs to have) in order to experience joy. Absolute power—the power to command everyone—is the extreme form of this joy; indeed, nothing less than this taste of heaven will serve to satisfy him. He will, he declares, "account this world but hell/Until my misshaped trunk that bears this head/Be round impaled with a glorious crown" (3.2.169–71).

Richard is well aware that he is trafficking in mere wish-fulfillment fantasy. His brother King Edward has two small sons who are the lineal heirs to the throne; and should neither of them chance to survive, there is also his older brother George, Duke of Clarence. There is a vast gulf between Richard and the crown he craves. "Why, then," he says,

> I do but dream on sovereignty
> Like one that stands upon a promontory
> And spies a far-off shore where he would tread,
> Wishing his foot were equal with his eye,
> And chides the sea that sunders him from thence,
> Saying he'll lade it dry to have his way.
>   (*3 Henry VI* 3.2.134–39)

There is something desperate and almost pathetic about this twisted man dreaming that he will one day have the power to push everyone around and, in doing so, compensate for his unloved, unbalanced body. He is, he ruefully acknowledges, like someone "lost in a thorny wood," tearing himself on the thorns and struggling in torment to find the open air.

In these circumstances, the principal weapon Richard has is the very absurdity of his ambition. No one in his right mind would suspect that he seriously aspires to the throne. And he is confident in his possession of one particular and, in his case, essential skill. He is a gifted deceiver. "Why, I can smile and murder whiles I smile," he says, congratulating himself,

> And cry "Content!" to that which grieves my heart,
> And wet my cheeks with artificial tears,
> And frame my face to all occasions. (3.2.182–85)

He has the special histrionic gifts of a confidence man.

In the spectacular opening soliloquy of *Richard III*, Richard reminds the audience where the trilogy had left off: "Now is the winter of our discontent/Made glorious summer by this son of York" (*Richard III* 1.1.1–2). Shakespeare then reopened the window into his character. England is at last at peace, but there is no peace for the twisted Duke of Gloucester. Everyone else can turn to the pursuit of pleasure:

> But I, that am not shaped for sportive tricks,
> Nor made to court an amorous looking glass;
> I, that am rudely stamped and want love's majesty
> To strut before a wanton ambling nymph;
> I, that am curtailed of this fair proportion,
> Cheated of feature by dissembling nature,
> Deformed, unfinished, sent before my time
> Into this breathing world scarce half made up,
> And that so lamely and unfashionable
> That dogs bark at me as I halt by them;
> Why, I, in this weak piping time of peace,
> Have no delight to pass away the time. (1.1.14–25)

"Deformed, unfinished, sent before my time/Into this breathing world scarce half made up," Richard will not attempt to be a lover but will instead pursue power by any means necessary.

Shakespeare did not suggest that a compensatory model— power as a substitute for sexual pleasure—could fully explain the psychology of a tyrant. But he held on to the core conviction that there is a significant relationship between the lust for tyrannical power and a thwarted or damaged psychosexual life. And he held on as well to the conviction that traumatic and lasting damage to a person's self-image could be traced back to early experiences—to an adolescent's fear that he is ugly, or to the cruel mockery of other children, or, even earlier in life, to the responses of nurses and midwives. Above all, he thought, irreparable harm could come from a mother's failure or inability to love her child. Richard's bitter anger at the goddess Love, who forswore him, and at nature, who shrank his arm like a withered shrub, is a thin screen for his rage against his mother.

Richard III is among the few plays in Shakespeare to depict a mother-child relationship. Far more often the plots focus upon children and their fathers—Egeus in *A Midsummer Night's Dream*, Henry IV in the two plays that bear his name, Leonato in *Much Ado About Nothing*, Brabantio in *Othello*, both Lear and Gloucester in *King Lear*, Prospero in *The Tempest*, to name only a few—with scarcely so much as a memory trace of the women who brought those children into the world. The *Henry VI* trilogy manages to feature York's four sons—Edward, George, Rutland, and Richard—without bothering to introduce their mother. The plays' emphasis is not on the individual or the family but on the whole realm's slide into civil war. When, however, Shakespeare focused on the character of the tyrant himself—the inward bitterness, disorder, and violence that drive him forward, to the ruin of his country—then he needed to explore something amiss in the relation between mother and child.

Richard's mother, the Duchess of York, makes it clear from her first appearance in *Richard III* that she regards her son as a monster. She has ample reason to do so. She does not know the details, but she suspects that Richard, and not her ailing elder son Edward, was behind the murder of their brother George. Richard has expressed great sympathy and love for his niece and nephew, George's orphaned children, but the duchess warns them—"shallow innocents," as she calls them—not to believe a word he says. "Think you my uncle did dissemble, grandam?" asks one of the children. "Ay, boy," she curtly replies. She expresses some combination of two contradictory sentiments, disgrace and disavowal. "He is my son, ay, and therein my shame," she acknowledges, and then immediately abjures any responsibility: "Yet from my dugs he drew not this deceit" (*Richard III* 2.2.18, 29–30). When the word is brought that Edward has died, leaving Richard as the sole survivor of her four sons, the duchess's feeling of disgrace is only intensified. "I for comfort have but one false glass [i.e. mirror]," she says with bitterness, "That grieves me when I see my shame in him" (2.2.53–54).

Richard arrives and puts on a show of filial piety, kneeling down for his mother's blessing. She complies stiffly, but it is clear that she is sickened by what she has brought into the world. Later in the play, she urges the other women whose lives her child has blighted—old Margaret, the widow of

Henry VI; Elizabeth, the widow of Edward; and Richard's miserably unhappy wife, Anne—to give vent to their grief and anger. "In the breath of bitter words," she tells them, "let's smother/My damnèd son" (4.4.133–34). When he appears before them, she first thinks to call him the word that encapsulates the revulsion his appearance has always aroused: "Thou toad, thou toad." If she had only strangled him in her womb, she tells him, she could have prevented all of the misery he has brought to the world and into her life:

> Thou cam'st on earth to make the earth my hell.
> A grievous burden was thy birth to me;
> Tetchy and wayward was thy infancy;
> Thy school days frightful, desperate, wild, and furious;
> Thy prime of manhood daring, bold, and venturous;
> Thy age confirmed proud, subtle, sly, and bloody.
> (4.4.167–72)

Declaring that she will never speak to him again, she finishes by cursing him and praying for his death: "Bloody thou art; bloody will be thy end."

The mother's shame and loathing are not merely a consequence of her son's wicked deeds; they reach all the way to the beginning, to her first glimpse of her newborn and to his tetchy and wayward infancy. Toward Edward and toward George she expresses maternal tenderness and solicitude; toward deformed Richard, she has always felt only disgust and aversion.

Richard's response, not surprisingly, is to order the sounding of trumpets and drums in order to drown out her curses. But the play manages to imply that his mother's rejection has reached him and implanted in him something more than impatience and rage. It implies, as well, that in response to this rejection, he has somehow developed lifelong strategies to make himself heard, attended to, and taken in. One of Richard's uncanny skills—and, in Shakespeare's view, one of the tyrant's most characteristic qualities—is the ability to force his way into the minds of those around him, whether they wish him there or not. It is as if, in compensation for the pain he has suffered, he has found a way to be present—by force or fraud, violence or insinuation—everywhere and in everyone. No one can keep him out.

Five

ENABLERS

RICHARD'S VILLAINY IS readily apparent to almost everyone. There is no deep secret about his cynicism, cruelty, and treacherousness, no glimpse of anything redeemable in him, and no reason to believe that he could ever govern the country effectively. The question the play explores, then, is how such a person actually attained the English throne. The achievement, Shakespeare suggests, depended on a fatal conjunction of diverse but equally self-destructive responses from those around him. Together these responses amount to a whole country's collective failure.

A few characters are genuinely fooled by Richard, crediting his claims, believing in his pledges, taking at face value his displays of emotion. Since there is little they can do to help or hinder Richard's rise—they are, for the most part, small children, and too innocent, naïve, or simply powerless to play a significant role in political life—they count merely among the dupes and victims.

There are also those who feel frightened or impotent in

the face of bullying and the menace of violence. "I'll make a corpse of him that disobeys" (*Richard III* 1.2.37), Richard threatens, and the opposition to his outrageous commands somehow shrivels away. It helps that he is an immensely wealthy and privileged man, accustomed to having his way, even when his way violates every moral norm.

Then there are those who cannot keep in focus that Richard is as bad as he seems to be. They know that he is a pathological liar and they see perfectly well that he has done this or that ghastly thing, but they have a strange penchant for forgetting, as if it were hard work to remember just how awful he is. They are drawn irresistibly to normalize what is not normal.

Another group is composed of those who do not quite forget that Richard is a miserable piece of work but who nonetheless trust that everything will continue in a normal way. They persuade themselves that there will always be enough adults in the room, as it were, to ensure that promises will be kept, alliances honored, and core institutions respected. Richard is so obviously and grotesquely unqualified for the supreme position of power that they dismiss him from their minds. Their focus is always on someone else, until it is too late. They fail to realize quickly enough that what seemed impossible is actually happening. They have relied on a structure that proves unexpectedly fragile.

A more sinister group consists of those who persuade themselves that they can take advantage of Richard's rise to power. Like almost everyone else, they see perfectly well how destructive he is, but they are confident that they will stay one step ahead of the tide of evil or manage to seize some profit from it. These allies and followers—Hastings, Catesby, and, above all, Buckingham—help him ascend from step to step, participating in his dirty work and watching the casualties mount with cool indifference. Some of these cynical collaborators, as Shakespeare imagines them, will be among the first to go under, once Richard has used them to obtain his end.

Finally, there a motley crowd of those who carry out his orders, some reluctantly but simply eager to avoid trouble; others with gusto, hoping to seize something along the way for themselves; still others enjoying the cruel game of making his targets, often high in the social hierarchy, suffer and die. The aspiring tyrant never lacks for such people, in Shakespeare and, from what I can tell, in life. True, there might be a world somewhere where this does not happen. Such is the world that Montaigne's friend Étienne de La Boétie once envisaged, where the dictator would fall simply because of a massive, nonviolent refusal to cooperate. He would call for some strawberries or for a round of executions, and no one would move a muscle. But Shakespeare seems to have regarded such a proto-Gandhian idea as hopeless pie in the sky. He thought that the tyrant would always find willing executioners, men who would, in Hamlet's phrase, "make love to this employment" (*Hamlet* 5.2.57).

Listing the types of enablers risks missing what is most compelling about Shakespeare's theatrical genius: not the construction of abstract categories or the calculation of degrees of complicity but the unforgettably vivid imagining of lived experience. Faced with the deep disturbance caused by Richard's ambition, grappling with confusing signals, and utterly uncertain of the outcome, people are forced to choose among flawed alternatives. *Richard III* brilliantly sketches men and women making anxious calculations under unbearable pressure and taking fateful decisions, conditioned by emotional currents beyond their rational control. It is the power of great theater to bring these dilemmas to life.

At the outer edge of complicity are those who, despite what they may have heard or even directly witnessed, still count on Richard's assurances. Such people find it almost impossible to resist the big, bold lie, shamelessly reiterated. The young and inexperienced are a relatively easy mark. When the murdered Clarence's son is told that his uncle Richard's show of grief is fraudulent, the child replies, "I cannot think it" (*Richard III* 2.2.31–33). "I cannot think it" serves as the motto for those who simply cannot get their minds around such perfidy. And what, after all, was the little orphaned boy to do with the cruel disillusionment his grandmother offered him?

Youth is not the only factor in fatal gullibility. Indeed, most conspicuous among those who trust Richard's fraudulent professions of friendship is not a child at all but, rather, his tough, experienced, and politically adroit older brother Clarence. Shakespeare's *Henry VI, Part 3* had depicted Clarence's strategic shifts in loyalty during the Wars of the Roses. He is therefore fully immersed in the web of hypocrisy, betrayal, and violence, and he has had every opportunity to see his dangerous brother in action. Why, when he is suddenly arrested and taken to the Tower, would Clarence credit Richard's offers of help?

The answers to this question take us to several key reasons why otherwise savvy political players could be tricked by so obvious a scoundrel, thereby making his wildly implausible rise to the throne possible. Events happen at a dizzying pace. "Plots have I laid," Richard discloses in his opening soliloquy,

> By drunken prophecies, libels, and dreams,
> To set my brother Clarence and the King
> In deadly hate the one against the other.
> (*Richard III* 1.1.32–36)

At the next moment, we see the guarded Clarence being led off to the Tower. In a brief conversation, under the eye of the jailor, Richard quickly promises sympathy and suggests that the imprisonment has been caused not by the king— who is, after all, their own brother—but by the king's wife. Clarence thus finds himself plunged into a frightening and complex political situation, one difficult to untangle. There is residual tension between himself and his brother Edward, whose rise to the throne Clarence had not fully supported. There is an entirely predictable jostling for power between the queen's family, on the one hand, and the king's family, on the other. There is also the king's mistress, Jane Shore, an independent influence, to reckon with. How, under the pressure of a rapidly unfolding crisis, is the prisoner sup- posed to sort it out? If he could imagine Richard's insane plan to kill off everyone between himself and the throne, it would all become clear, but without that key, everything is murky.

Richard dangles the lure of fraternal solidarity: "We are not safe, Clarence, we are not safe" (1.1.70). And Clarence rises to take it, counting on the primacy of such basic human instincts as family loyalty. We know that it would have been far safer to throw himself on the mercy of the king or the queen or the king's mistress, but in this swirling confusion he has no way of seeing clearly. His mind, as we shortly learn, is further clouded by guilt, his awareness of the moral compromises he has made in the past. He is hardly alone: in Shakespeare's play, there are almost no morally uncompromised lives. Virtually everyone grapples with painful memories of lies and broken vows, memories that make it all the more difficult for them to grasp where the deepest danger lies.

And yet Clarence does, after all, have an intimation of the mortal danger that resides in Gloucester (as he calls his brother Richard, Duke of Gloucester); the problem is that this intimation resides only in his dreams. In a remarkable scene in the Tower, the prisoner awakens from a miserable night's fitful sleep and tells the jailor about a terrible dream he has just had. It began, he recalls, with a fantasy of escape:

> Methoughts that I had broken from the Tower
> And was embarked to cross to Burgundy,
> And in my company my brother Gloucester,

Who from my cabin tempted me to walk
Upon the hatches. (1.4.9–13)

At this point, the dream plunged abruptly into nightmare:

As we paced along
Upon the giddy footing of the hatches,
Methought that Gloucester stumbled, and in falling
Struck me, that thought to stay him, overboard
Into the tumbling billows of the main.
O Lord, methought what pain it was to drown.
    (1.4.16–21)

It is almost all there: in his subconscious, Clarence grasps
that his brother keeps himself upright by striking down those
around him and even that his brother will be the cause of his
death. What is missing however, is a grasp of either Richard's malevolence or his motive. In the dream, it is simply a
horrible accident.

A few minutes later, not in a dream but in broad waking,
two thugs hired by Richard appear in the Tower. Assuming
that they have been dispatched by his brother Edward, Clarence reverts to his delusional trust. "I will send you to my
brother Gloucester," he tells the thugs, "Who shall reward
you better for my life/Than Edward will for tidings of my
death." "You are deceived," one of them informs him. "Your
brother Gloucester hates you." This terrible truth Clarence
absolutely refuses to believe: "Oh, no, he loves me, and he

holds me dear./Go you to him from me." Replying with grim humor, "Ay, so we will" (1.4.221–26), the assassin stabs Clarence, then drowns him in a wine barrel, after which he hurries off to Richard for his reward.

In hindsight, Clarence's dream had a horrible premonitory power, extending to the detail of his death by drowning, but its significance reaches beyond this local irony. It reveals something broadly important about tyranny on the rise: its frightening ability to penetrate the mind in sleep, even as it can also penetrate the body. In *Richard III*, dreams are not decorative touches or mere glimpses of individual psychology. They are essential to an understanding of a tyrant's power to exist in and as everyone's nightmare. And the tyrant has the power to make nightmares real.

It is only in a dream that Clarence can see what his brother actually intends. Waking, and even confronted by the killers themselves, he cannot bring himself to accept that he has been betrayed by someone who "bewept my fortune,/And hugged me in his arms, and swore with sobs/ That he would labor my delivery" (1.4.235–37). Not everyone in the play is so defended against the truth hidden in dreams. At four a.m., a messenger beats at the door of the powerful Lord Hastings to report that Lord Stanley has had a nightmare: "He dreamt the boar had razed off his helm" (3.2.10)—that is, Stanley has dreamed that Richard cut off his head. Hastings dismisses the omen. "Tell him his fears are shallow," he instructs the messenger. "And for his dreams, I wonder he's so simple/To trust the mock'ry of unquiet slumbers" (3.2.24–26). To run away in panic would only be to excite suspicion:

> To fly the boar before the boar pursues
> Were to incense the boar to follow us
> And make pursuit where he did mean no chase.
>   (3.2.27–29)

It is safer, Hastings counsels, to stay put. As it turns out, it is the fearful Stanley who in the end manages to save his own life, while Hastings winds up with his head chopped off.

But why would Hastings, who has observed Richard's ruthlessness from up close, allow himself to fall into the trap? The answer is that ambitious Hastings thinks that he can take advantage of this ruthlessness to rid himself of his principal rivals at court. He is not ignorant of the potential risk, but he believes that he has adequately defended himself against it, both by making himself useful to Richard in the past and by cultivating well-placed allies who can warn him if the wind seemed to be shifting in an alarming direction. The chief of these allies is "my good friend Catesby,/Where nothing can proceed that toucheth us/Whereof I shall not have intelligence" (3.2.21–23).

What Hastings fails to grasp is that his informant Catesby, watching out for his own interests, may be less securely in his pocket than he imagines. A conversation immediately follows in which Catesby, bringing news that several of Hastings's enemies have just gone to their deaths, sounds out his willingness to support Richard's attempt to seize the throne. Loyal to the young son of the late king, Hastings stoutly declines, having no idea that his refusal seals his fate; he is thinking only of his enemies' downfall. He anticipates further triumphs of self-interest in the weeks to come, triumphs that will all stem from his friendship and collaboration with Richard: "Well, Catesby, ere a fortnight make me older,/I'll send some packing that yet think not on't" (3.2.59–60). But, of course, it is he who is sent packing. In a terrifying scene, Richard dispatches him as if he were a nuisance to be eliminated before lunch: "Off with his head! Now, by Saint Paul, I swear/I will not dine until I see the same" (3.4.75–77).

The tyrant gives the order, but he obviously does not carry it out himself. And his collaborators include far more than the man with an axe; the room in which Richard issues his command is full of powerful people sitting around a table. Stanley—he of the bad dream—is there, along with the Duke of Buckingham, the Bishop of Ely, Sir Richard Ratcliffe, Sir Francis Lovell, the Duke of Norfolk, and others. They have all known Hastings for years, and they all know that the treason charge brought against him—using witchcraft to wither Richard's arm—is utterly absurd, Richard's arm having been deformed from birth. Some, like Buckingham and Catesby, are already in on the plot to take Hastings's life; others, like Ratcliffe and Lovell, are happy to go along with anything the tyrant orders; still others are simply relieved that the blade of the axe is not pointed in their direction.

All must bear some responsibility, even those who merely

remain silent and imagine that they are therefore free from blame. Earlier in the play, the Lieutenant of the Tower, Sir Robert Brakenbury, receives a written directive that he turn over his prisoner Clarence to the two thuggish-looking characters. One glance makes clear their intention. Brakenbury knows perfectly well that his prisoner has not received a trial, fair or otherwise, but, handing the keys to the murderers, he asks no questions and offers no protest: "I will not reason what is meant hereby/Because I will be guiltless from the meaning" (1.4.93–94). By multiple acts of this kind, taken by respectable people eager to be "guiltless from the meaning," tyranny is enabled.

A succession of murders clears the field of most of the significant impediments, actual or potential, to Richard's seizing power. But it is striking that Shakespeare does not envisage the tyrant's climactic accession to the throne as the direct result of violence. Instead, it is the consequence of an election. To solicit a popular mandate, Richard conducts a political campaign, complete with a fraudulent display of religious piety, the slandering of opponents, and a grossly exaggerated threat to national security.

Why an election? Adherence to his sources, especially Thomas More's *The History of King Richard III*, is not a sufficient explanation. Shakespeare felt comfortable trimming and making changes whenever it suited him. (The play compresses events that in reality occurred over a long period of time, so that, for example, Richard's murderous plot against his brother Clarence [1478] is cleverly twined around his cynical courtship of Lady Anne [1472], which is, in turn, depicted as occurring during the funeral procession of King Henry [1471].) Since Elizabethans lived their lives in a hereditary—not elective—monarchy, it might have made sense for Shakespeare to downplay or eliminate this part of the story, as he found it in More. But instead he placed the election scene at the center of his play.

The "citizens"—the ordinary people—have heard rumors that king has died, leaving the crown to his young son, under the guidance of the child's uncles. To people who have always had good reason to be nervous about regime change, none of this augers well: "Woe to that land that's governed by a child" (2.3.12), says one. Ordinarily, there is precious little that simple subjects can do beyond bracing themselves for whatever will come. Notes this same bystander: "When clouds are seen, wise men put on their cloaks" (2.3.33). But in this case, they are drawn into a complex political game, one in which they will be asked to overthrow the order of succession, reject the king's son, and elect Richard instead.

With the aid of Buckingham, who serves, in effect, as his chief strategist and campaign manager, Richard begins by fabricating a lie about how they have foiled a treasonous plot by Hastings to topple the government. Only quick action, culminating in the summary execution of the traitor, has saved the state. Under the emergency circumstances, Richard tells London's Lord Mayor, there could be no public airing of evidence and no "form of law." When Hastings's severed head is brought in, Buckingham explains that, had it not been for the "loving haste" of the patriots who beheaded him, the mayor would have heard for himself the traitor freely confess his crimes and could have verified the whole story to the citizens. "Your graces' words," the compliant mayor assures them, "shall serve/As well as I had seen and heard him speak" (3.5.62–63).

Richard and his henchman pride themselves on being gifted actors who can easily perform the part of men who have narrowly escaped from a fiendish plot. "Tut, I can counterfeit the deep tragedian," Buckingham boasts,

> Speak, and look back, and pry on every side,
> Tremble and start at wagging of a straw,
> Intending deep suspicion. (3.5.5–8)

And they are gifted, as well, at conveying just the right blend of friendliness and menace needed to enlist the cooperation of civic officials like the mayor. But it is not at all clear that the performance actually fools anyone. A moment after the exchange with the mayor, Shakespeare includes a very short scene—only fourteen lines long—in which a nameless scribe mutters about a legal document he has just copied. The document is the indictment of Hastings, and, reflecting on the time line, the scribe easily grasps that the charges were concocted well in advance, while Hastings was still "Untainted, unexamined, free, at liberty" (3.6.9). The whole business is a lie, to cover the extrajudicial murder of one of Richard's enemies. "Who is so gross/That cannot see this palpable device?" the scribe asks. "Yet who so bold but says he sees it not?" (3.6.10–12).

What is the point, then, of the elaborate rigmarole—not only the alleged treasonous conspiracy and the backdated indictment but also Richard's masquerade of piety, his professed reluctance to rule, the fraudulent suggestion that the child king is illegitimate, and all the rest of the lies? It is not just the scribe who sees through the fraud. The first attempt to solicit popular support for Richard's ascendency is a failure: the voters simply do not comply. On the contrary, Buckingham reports, "they spake not a word,/But like dumb statues or breathing stones/ Stared each on other and looked deadly pale" (3.7.24–26).

Yet if the lies hardly produce robust consent, they nonetheless have some effect. The steady barrage of falsehoods plays its part, working to marginalize skeptics, to sow confusion, to quiet protests that might otherwise have erupted. Whether from indifference or from fear or from the catastrophically mistaken belief that there is no real difference between Richard and the alternatives, the citizens fail to resist. Indeed, a second attempt to solicit their votes is more successful. Buckingham's "Long live king Richard, England's worthy king!" is met with the cry "Amen" (3.7.238–39).

Shakespeare himself may have had some difficulty deciding how much popular support there actually was for the tyrant's ascent. There are two texts of *Richard III* both of which can claim authority. In the Quarto, a small, inexpensive edition published during the playwright's lifetime, only the Lord Mayor shouts "Amen" to Buckingham's "Love live

Richard!" (Quarto 3.7.218–19). But in the Folio, brought out seven years after Shakespeare's death, the speech prefix for the decisive "Amen" is "All" (Folio 3.7.238–39). In one version, then, it is only the tyrant's shill who voices consent; in the other version, it is the whole crowd.

The ambiguity seems built into Shakespeare's conception of Richard. Notwithstanding his ugliness, does he have some allure? Is there a moment in which the crowd actually supports him, or is it only a conspiracy? Are his lies somehow still effective, even though people see through them? The election is only the climax of the strange tightrope act that is performed almost from the beginning, most notably in a famous scene in which Richard forces himself on Lady Anne, the person in the world least likely to succumb to his blandishments. Lady Anne has every reason to hate Richard, who has, as Shakespeare stages it, killed both her young husband and his father, King Henry VI. When the murderer woos her—quite literally—over Henry VI's dead body, Anne curses him, spitting in his face in a visceral expression of loathing and disgust. But by the end of the scene, she has accepted Richard's ring and, in effect, agreed to marry him.

Actors can play the scene in radically different ways. Vulnerable and powerless in the presence of a monster, Anne has almost no choice. Alternatively, though she loathes and fears Richard, Anne can seem strangely fascinated by him, aroused somehow even in the midst of their most aggressive exchanges. At the end of their intense back-and-forth, after steadily expressing her contempt for his professions of love,

Anne finds herself not cursing but musing: "I would I knew thy heart" (1.2.192). For his part, when she exits, Richard exults, "Was ever woman in this humor wooed?/Was ever woman in this humor won?" (1.2.267–68). There is not a shred of tenderness or truth in anything he has said; "I'll have her," he coolly reflects, "but I will not keep her long" (1.2.228). Richard is incapable of love, and he will soon do away with her, as he promises. But his power, wealth, and sheer brazenness permit him to seize upon someone he wants, even someone who finds him repellent. It counts for him as pleasure.

Where is the audience in relation to this spectacle, part rape, part seduction? To the extent that the actor evinces anything other than sheer disgust, Anne exhibits the peculiar excitement that Richard arouses in most spectators. The play does not encourage a rational identification with Richard's political goal, but it does awaken a certain complicity in its audience, the complicity of those who take vicarious pleasure in the release of pent-up aggression, in the black humor of it all, in the open speaking of the unspeakable. "Your eyes drop millstones when fools' eyes fall tears," Richard says to the men he has hired to kill his own brother. "I like you, lads" (1.3.352–53).

Within the play, Richard's rise is made possible by various degrees of complicity from those around him. But in the theater, it is we, the audience, watching it all happening, who are lured into a peculiar form of collaboration. We are charmed again and again by the villain's outrageousness, by his indifference to the ordinary norms of human decency, by lies that seem to be effective even though no one believes them. Looking out at us from the stage, Richard invites us not only to share his gleeful contempt but also to experience for ourselves what it is to succumb to what we know to be loathsome.

In his jaunty wickedness and perverse humor, Richard has seduced more than four centuries of audiences. One of the rare anecdotes that survive from Shakespeare's time suggests that this seduction began almost immediately. In 1602 a London law student, John Manningham, recorded a ribald story in his diary:

> Upon a time when Burbage played Richard III there was a citizen grew so far in liking with him, that before she went from the play she appointed him to come that night unto her by the name of Richard III. Shakespeare, overhearing their conclusion, went before, was entertained and at his game ere Burbage came. The message being brought that Richard III was at the door, Shakespeare caused return to be made that William the Conqueror was before Richard III.[18]

Like most stories about celebrities, this one probably says more about those who circulated it than about those it describes. But it does at least suggest that Richard Burbage, the famous actor who first played Richard III (as well as such parts as Romeo and Hamlet), had not by virtue of his villainous role lost all of his glamour.

From the start, the play seems to have aroused intense interest: first performed in 1592 or 1593, *Richard III* was published in quarto no fewer than five times during Shakespeare's lifetime. Its villain—the "elvish-marked, abortive, rooting hog" (1.3.267), the "poisonous bunch-backed toad" (1.3.245), the heartless cur sent, as he himself puts it, "deformed" and "unfinished" (1.1.20) into the world—has seemed weirdly and compellingly attractive to generations of actors, playgoers, and readers. Something in us enjoys every minute of his horrible ascent to power.

Six

TYRANNY
TRIUMPHANT

THERE IS A TOUCH of comedy in the tyrant's rise to power, catastrophe though it is. The people he has pushed aside and trampled on are for the most part themselves compromised, cynical, or corrupt. Even if their fates are ghastly, it is satisfying to see them get their comeuppance, and as we watch the schemer bluster and connive and betray his way to the top, we are invited to take a kind of moral vacation.

But once Richard reaches his lifelong goal—at the end of the third act of Shakespeare's play—the laughter quickly begins to curdle. Much of the pleasure of his winning derived from its wild improbability. Now the prospect of endless winning proves to be a grotesque delusion. Though he has seemed a miracle of dark efficiency, Richard is quite unprepared to unite and run a whole country.

The tyrant's triumph is based on lies and fraudulent promises braided around the violent elimination of rivals. The cunning strategy that brings him to the throne hardly constitutes a vision for the realm; nor has he assembled counselors who can help him formulate one. He can count—for the moment, at least—on the acquiescence of such suggestible officials as the London mayor and frightened clerks like the scribe. But the new ruler possesses neither administrative ability nor diplomatic skill, and no one in his entourage can supply what he manifestly lacks. His own mother despises him. His wife, Anne, fears and hates him. Cynical operators like Catesby and Ratcliffe are hardly suited to be statesmen. Though higher in social station, they differ little from the hoodlums Richard hires to do his bidding. Lord Stanley cuts a more plausible figure as a prudent adviser—and the play depicts him reluctantly conveying the king's wishes—but, as his early nightmare suggests, he has long been afraid of "the boar" and can hardly be expected to serve as a linchpin of the upstart regime. Secretly he is already in contact with the regime's mortal enemies.

The most plausible candidate to help uphold Richard's reign is his long-term ally, kinsman, and partner in crime, the Duke of Buckingham. The canny duke was the mastermind behind Richard's successful political campaign and assisted in the destruction of a succession of real or imagined enemies. "Thus high by thy advice/And thy assistance," the newly enthroned tyrant tells Buckingham, "is King Richard seated" (*Richard III* 4.2.3–4). This acknowledgment of indebtedness, however, is a prelude to a further request for advice and assistance.

Though he has carefully sent everyone else out of ear-shot, Richard is at first somewhat coy about what he wants. "Young Edward lives," he notes, referring to the late king's heir, who is being held along with his cousin in the Tower; "think now what I would speak" (4.2.10). But Buckingham steadfastly refuses to play the guessing game, whose meaning is not difficult to divine. Richard, increasingly vexed, is forced to make his meaning clear:

> Cousin, thou wast not wont to be so dull.
> Shall I be plain? I wish the bastards dead,
> And I would have it suddenly performed.
> What say'st thou? Speak suddenly. Be brief.
>
> (4.2.17–20)

Buckingham's reply is a model of brevity—"Your grace may do your pleasure"—but it still does not give the tyrant what he wants. Again he is forced to put the question more directly than he would have wished: "Say, have I thy consent that they shall die?" Before slipping out of the room, Buckingham once again avoids providing a direct answer: "Give me some little breath, some pause, my lord,/Before I positively speak in this" (4.2.21–24).

Richard is not asking Buckingham to murder the little children himself; for that he knows he can and will easily find the appropriate killer. And Buckingham is right that Richard does not need anyone's permission. That the tyrant asks his principal ally for his "consent" has to do not with permission but with complicity. At this critical moment at the onset of his reign, he wants and needs to be assured of his associate's loyalty, and that loyalty is best guaranteed by having Buckingham make himself an accomplice to a horrendous crime. Though it would have been still better if Buckingham had suggested on his own that the children be killed—hence Richard's initial coyness—the associate's simple "consent" will serve as a sufficient guarantee. Buckingham, however, is evasive, and Richard is vexed. "The King is angry," remarks Catesby, who has been watching from a distance. "See, he gnaws his lip" (4.2.27).

The brief exchange introduces several key features of the tyrant's rule, as Shakespeare envisaged it. For the tyrant, there is remarkably little satisfaction. True, he has obtained the position to which he aspired, but the skills that enabled him to do so are not at all the same as those required to govern successfully. Whatever pleasures he might have imagined would be his give way to frustration, anger, and gnawing fear. Moreover, the possession of power is never secure. There is always something else that must be done in order to reinforce his position, and since he has reached his goal through criminal acts, what is required inevitably are further criminal acts. The tyrant is obsessed with loyalty from his inner circle, but he can never be entirely confident that he has it. The only people who will serve him are self-interested scoundrels, like himself; in any case, he has no interest in honest loyalty or dispassionate, independent judgment. Instead he wants flattery, confirmation, and obedience.

"Yond Cassius has a lean and hungry look," Shakespeare's Julius Caesar famously remarks. "He thinks too much; such men are dangerous" (*Julius Caesar* 1.2.194–95). Antony attempts to reassure him—"He's not dangerous"—but Caesar is unconvinced: "He reads much,/He is a great observer, and he looks/Quite through the deeds of men" (1.2.196, 201–3). These are not qualities that men like Caesar want anywhere near them: "Let me have men about me that are fat,/Sleek-headed men, and such as sleep a-nights" (1.2.192–93).

Standing at the pinnacle of his world, Richard reaches the same conclusion: "None are for me,/That look into me with considerate"—that is, carefully thoughtful—"eyes" (*Richard III* 4.2.29–30). Buckingham, he reflects, "grows circumspect" (4.2.31), and circumspection is potentially dangerous. When, after his pause for reflection, Buckingham returns, Richard waves him off; he is no longer interested in whether he has his "consent" or not. And when his old ally then repeatedly asks for the reward that he had been promised for his many services, Richard peremptorily dismisses him: "Thou troublest me. I am not in the vein" (4.2.99). Having participated in the entrapment and betrayal of so many others, Buckingham is able to read the ominous signs very clearly and decides to flee for his life. His effort is in vain; he will eventually be caught and executed.

Now that he has decided that he can no longer risk sharing his secrets with his former confidant, Richard is faced with making key tactical moves on his own. He needs, as he puts it, "To stop all hopes whose growth may damage me"

(4.2.59). The tyrant is, in effect, the enemy of hope. He finds a "discontented gentleman," down on his luck and willing to do anything for "corrupting gold," to arrange for the killing of the two royal children (4.2.36–39). Their deaths will leave alive only a single heir to the deceased King Edward, a young daughter, and Richard calculates that by marrying her, he will shore up his fragile authority. "Murder her brothers, and then marry her," he broods. "Uncertain way of gain" (4.2.62–63). Uncertain it may be, but without it, as he puts it to himself, "my kingdom stands on brittle glass" (4.2.61). Of course, he is already married, but he instructs Catesby to begin to rumor it abroad that Queen Anne is ill. When even the ever-serviceable Catesby hesitates for a moment, Richard bristles with impatience: "Look how thou dream'st! I say again, give out/That Anne my queen is sick and like to die" (4.2.56–57).

Impatience is another of the qualities that, in Shakespeare's view, inevitably marks the tyrant's experience of power. He expects his wishes to be carried out almost before he has expressed them aloud. New developments keep arising, most of them alarming, and time is no longer a friend. Delay is dangerous; everything has to be done in haste, with scarcely a moment to think. Once ruthlessly efficient, Richard begins to seem distracted, as in this rushed exchange with his two principal accomplices:

> KING RICHARD: Some light-foot friend post to the
>   Duke of Norfolk:
>   Ratcliffe, thyself, or Catesby. Where is he?

CATESBY: Here, my good lord.

KING RICHARD: Catesby, fly to the Duke.

CATESBY: Here, my good lord.

KING RICHARD: Ratcliffe, come hither. Post to
    Salisbury.
When thou com'st thither—[to CATESBY] Dull,
    unmindful villain,
Why stay'st thou here and go'st not to the Duke?

CATESBY: First, mighty liege, tell me your highness'
    pleasure,
What from your grace I shall deliver to him.

KING RICHARD: Oh, true, good Catesby. Bid him
    levy straight
The greatest strength and power that he can make,
And meet me suddenly at Salisbury. [Exit CATESBY.]
    (4.4.440–451)

A moment later he displays a similar blend of impatience and incompetence with Ratcliffe, and still the disquieting news keeps flooding in upon him. An invasion fleet has been glimpsed off the coast. A powerful nobleman, reports a messenger, is assembling forces against him in one part of the country; a different enemy, says another, is massing troops in a second area. In a paroxysm of frustration, Richard strikes yet another messenger, who he thinks has brought him further cause for alarm. "Take that," the king shouts "until thou bring me better news" (4.4.422). But the news in this case happens to be good. Even a beleaguered tyrant gets an occasional break.

While all of this is going on, Richard continues with his plan to marry his young niece, and in doing so he reveals a further feature that Shakespeare associated with tyranny: utter shamelessness. Though he has caused the murder of her two sons, he has the fathomless effrontery to approach Elizabeth, the widow of the late king, and propose that he marry her daughter. He does not even bother to deny his crime; instead, he proposes to repair the loss of her children by giving her grandchildren!

> If I have killed the issue of your womb,
> To quicken your increase I will beget
> Mine issue of your blood upon your daughter.
> (4.6.296–98)

Elizabeth's nausea and loathing do not faze him in the slightest. He simply forges ahead with his indecent proposal and his lies, confident that he can get away with anything. "Thou didst kill my children," she repeats, and Richard's confident response makes the sick perversity of what he is offering still more explicit:

> But in your daughter's womb I bury them
> Where, in that nest of spicery, they will breed
> Selves of themselves. (4.6.423–25)

When, to escape from him, Elizabeth agrees to speak to her daughter about the offer, Richard is convinced that he has again won, as he had earlier overmastered Anne's hatred. He can, he thinks, grab from any woman anything he wants, however much she might resist, and the thought produces in him a burst of misogynistic contempt: "Relenting fool, and shallow changing woman!" (4.6.431). But it is precisely at this point that the noose begins to tighten around the tyrant's neck. Elizabeth has no intention of giving her daughter to Richard; she is already in communication with Richard's principal enemy, the Earl of Richmond, who is leading the invasion force that will cast the tyrant down from the summit he should never have been permitted to climb.

In a scene on the eve of the Battle of Bosworth Field— the decisive military encounter that ends in Richmond's triumph and Richard's death—Shakespeare provides a glimpse of one further quality he associates with the tyrant: an absolute loneliness. With his henchmen Catesby and Ratcliffe, Richard can review battle plans and give orders, but he has no real closeness to them or to anyone else. He has long been aware that no one loves him and that no one will grieve his loss. "If I die," he admits to himself, "no soul will pity me" (5.3.201). Why should they, he adds, "since that I myself/ Find in myself no pity to myself?" (5.3.202–3). In his dreams, Richard is haunted by the ghosts of those he has betrayed and killed. They stand, in effect, for the conscience he conspicuously lacks. But he bears the most terrible burden— the burden of self-loathing—when he is fully awake and by himself.

At this fairly early stage in his career, Shakespeare had

not yet invented an entirely convincing way of representing a conflicted inner life. The soliloquy he gives Richard takes the form of a rather stiff interior dialogue, as if between two quarreling puppets:

> What do I fear? Myself? There's none else by.
> Richard loves Richard; that is, I am I.
> Is there a murderer here? No. Yes, I am.
> Then fly. What, from myself? Great reason why?
> Lest I revenge. What, myself upon myself?
> Alack, I love myself. Wherefore? For any good
> That I myself have done unto myself?
> Oh, no. Alas, I rather hate myself. (5.3.182–89)

In a very few years, Shakespeare would invent the inwardness he confers on Brutus, Hamlet, Macbeth, and others, and he never returned to the kind of writing he did here. But perhaps Richard's schematic words manage to convey the notion not only of psychological conflict—I love myself; I hate myself—but also of a painful emptiness. It is as if we look inside the tyrant and find that there is virtually nothing there, merely a few shrunken traces of a self that had never been allowed to grow or to flourish.

IN 2012, WORKERS constructing a parking lot in the English Midlands city of Leicester unearthed a decaying coffin that contained a human skeleton. Radiocarbon dating combined with clever genetic studies of known modern descendants of the York family revealed that the corpse in question was that of Richard III. There was a rush of media attention. One hundred and forty registered journalists and camera crews from seven countries crowded together for a press conference at the University of Leicester and then were solemnly ushered into a room. There, laid out decorously on a black velvet cloth draped over four library tables pushed together, were the bones of the king who reigned from 1483 until his battlefield death two years later, at the age of thirty-two.

In Shakespeare's play, Richard's horse is killed beneath him—"A horse, a horse, my kingdom for a horse!" (5.4.7), he repeatedly shouts—and, failing to get a new mount, he ranges on foot across the battlefield, looking to meet his enemy Richmond. When they finally encounter one another, they engage in single combat, and Richard is killed. "The day is ours," Richmond declares. "The bloody dog is dead" (5.5.2). In historical reality, as the bones that unexpectedly surfaced in the construction site bore witness, Richard's end took a somewhat different form. The base of Richard's skull had been shattered by a violent blow, probably from a halberd, that particularly gruesome two-handed pole weapon favored by late medieval soldiers. The king had thus presumably been killed from behind, and his bones show signs of what are called "humiliation injuries," that is, stab wounds through the buttocks and elsewhere that the victors must have inflicted on his corpse in a frenzy of loathing. But perhaps the most interesting piece of evidence brought to light after more than five hundred years is the spine, curved in a startling *S*. The physical deformation vividly conjured up the figure who actually accounted for the worldwide press coverage—not the relatively minor historical Richard but the unforgettable tyrant Shakespeare created and unleashed onto the London stage.

Seven

THE INSTIGATOR

ALMOST FIFTEEN YEARS after he wrote *Richard III*, Shakespeare returned to his vision of the twisted self that is at once the motive and the burden of tyrannical power. Drenched in blood from his treacherous assassination of Duncan to his miserable, despairing end, Macbeth is Shakespeare's most celebrated and memorable tyrant. But now the loneliness, self-loathing, and emptiness at the center of the tyrant's being have nothing to do with physical deformity. Macbeth does not use power to compensate for his lack of sexual attractiveness; he does not seethe with barely suppressed rage; he has not learned from childhood to disguise his actual feelings beneath a fraudulent mask of warmth or piety. And, strangely enough, he does not even wholeheartedly wish to be the king.

Unlike Richard, Macbeth has harbored no long-term dream of surmounting all obstacles and attaining absolute power. The Weird Sisters' uncanny greeting—"All hail, Macbeth, that shalt be king hereafter!" (*Macbeth*

1.3.51)—startles him, but initially it is a shock of fear rather than desire. For if Richard prides himself on his indifference to moral obligations and ordinary human feelings— "Tear-falling pity dwells not in this eye" (4.2.63)—Macbeth is highly sensitive to them. He is a stalwart, trusted military leader, a loyal defender of King Duncan's regime. When the hapless Duncan decides to visit him, Macbeth, though tantalized by the treasonous fantasy awakened in him, is appalled at the thought of betraying a guest in his own house, a ruler to whom he has sworn allegiance, who has rewarded him handsomely for his services, and who has exercised his authority with exemplary probity.

King Duncan, Macbeth reflects,

> Hath borne his faculties so meek, hath been
> So clear in his great office, that his virtues
> Will plead like angels, trumpet-tongued, against
> The deep damnation of his taking-off;
> And Pity, like a naked newborn babe
> Striding the blast, or heaven's cherubim horsed
> Upon the sightless couriers of the air,
> Shall blow the horrid deed in every eye,
> That tears shall drown the wind. (1.7.17–25)

These words, spoken only to himself and in deep anguish, are at the farthest remove from anything that could ever pass the lips of Richard III. We are in a different psychological and moral universe.

The very idea of killing a man to whom he has sworn allegiance causes Macbeth's hair to stand on end, his heart to pound with anxiety, and his mind to swirl in wild confusion:

> My thought, whose murder yet is but fantastical,
> Shakes so my single state of man
> That function is smothered in surmise,
> And nothing is but what is not. (1.3.141–44)

Though he is a fearless warrior, accustomed to cutting his enemies open "from the nave to the chops," simply contemplating treason makes him feel that he is falling apart.

The real instigator of the murder plot is not Macbeth but, rather, his wife. She anticipates resistance, for she knows her husband well and fears that he lacks key elements of the tyrannical personality. His nature is "too full o' th' milk of human kindness" (1.5.15) to do what has to be done. It is she who comes up with plans for what she calls "This night's great business" (1.5.66); she who instructs her husband how to comport himself; she who plies the royal bedroom attendants with drink. Macbeth remains full of doubt and hesitation. After all, Duncan is the king; and Macbeth, his host, "should against his murderer shut the door,/Not bear the knife myself" (1.7.15–16).

As the fatal hour approaches, he attempts to call off the plot—"We will proceed no further in this business" (1.7.31)—and it is only his wife's mocking insistence that persuades him to continue. "Was the hope drunk/Wherein you dressed yourself?" she asks him. "Art thou afeard/To be the same in thine own act and valor/As thou art in desire?" (1.7.35–36, 39–41). Macbeth tries to counter the imputation of weakness: "I dare do all that may become a man" (1.7.46). But his wife drives home the sexual point: "When you durst do it, then you were a man," she informs him. "And to be more than what you were, you would/Be so much more the man" (1.7.49–51). So provoked, he rises to the murderous occasion.

Lady Macbeth's gibes about her husband's manhood—his ability to be the same in act as he is in desire—bring up to the surface a recurrent implication in Shakespearean tyranny. The tyrant, *Macbeth* and other plays suggest, is driven by a range of sexual anxieties: a compulsive need to prove his manhood, dread of impotence, a nagging apprehension that he will not be found sufficiently attractive or powerful, a fear of failure. Hence the penchant for bullying, the vicious misogyny, and the explosive violence. Hence, too, the vulnerability to taunts, especially those bearing a latent or explicit sexual charge.

From the moment the Weird Sisters greeted him, Macbeth has been the embodiment of ambivalence, but his wife ruthlessly insists that he has irrevocably committed himself and cannot now back away:

> I have given suck and know
> How tender 'tis to love the babe that milks me;
> I would, while it was smiling in my face,

Have plucked my nipple from his boneless gums
And dashed the brains out, had I so sworn as you
Have done to this. (1.7.54–59)

Propelled against his better judgment toward the treasonous action, he expresses one last, desperate reservation—"If we should fail?"—but his wife turns the question back at him with yet another goad:

We fail?
But screw your courage to the sticking-place,
And we'll not fail. (1.7.59–61)

Macbeth's response is a startling one: "Bring forth men-children only," he tells her. "For thy undaunted mettle should compose/Nothing but males" (1.7.72–74). From this point on, having in effect accepted the role conferred upon him by his wife, his fate is sealed: "I am settled" (1.7.79), he says. We have watched the birth of the tyrant.

Once the deed is done, once Macbeth attains the "sovereign sway and masterdom" (1.5.68) that his wife had urged upon him, the psychological and moral abyss that separated him from Richard begins rapidly to close. He who had been appalled at the very thought of treachery now hires murderers to destroy his closest friend. He who had once been "valor's minion" (1.2.19), a man utterly without fear, is suddenly afraid of everything: "Whence is that knocking?/How is't with me when every noise appalls me?" (2.2.60–61). He who had been hard-pressed to disguise whatever he was thinking—"Your face," his wife complained to him, "is as a book where men/ May read strange matters" (1.5.60–61)—is now enmeshed in deceit and lies.

As with Richard's lies, no one quite believes them. "To show an unfelt sorrow" Duncan's eldest son, Malcolm, whispers to his brother, "is an office/Which the false man does easy" (2.3.133–34). "Where we are," his brother agrees, "There's daggers in men's smiles" (2.3.136–37). Like the wary survivors in Richard's realm, they both flee for their lives.

Those who stay in Scotland rehearse the official story Macbeth has put out: that Duncan was murdered by his personal attendants, set on to do so by the two sons who have now fled. The attendants cannot be questioned, because Macbeth—carried away, he says, by his "violent love" for the slain king—has killed them. For the new regime, it is a convenient fiction, enabling, as it does, the official ceremonies that confer a veneer of legitimacy on his rule. Tyrannical power is more easily exercised when it appears that the old order continues to exist. The reassuring consensual structures may now be hollowed out and merely decorative, but they are all still in place, so that the bystanders, who crave psychological security and a sense of well-being, can persuade themselves that the rule of law is being upheld.

Macbeth's friend Banquo, in any case, understands what is happening. He was present for the eerie prophecies on the heath, and he has been watching as each piece falls into place. "Thou hast it now," he muses about his friend. "King,

Cawdor, Glamis, all/As the weird women promised, and I fear/Thou play'dst most foully for't" (3.1.1–3). But, though he is a man of principle, Banquo neither speaks out nor runs away. He is not an enabler, like Buckingham, but he is Macbeth's ally, and he has no proof that what he merely suspects is true. Moreover, the prophecies extended to himself as well: "Thou shalt get [i.e., beget] kings, though thou be none" (1.3.68). If all that the Weird Sisters foresaw for Macbeth has proved true, then why, he asks himself, "May they not be my oracles as well/And set me up in hope?" (3.1.9–10).

The relationship between the friends has changed. Macbeth still speaks warmly to him, as if their old intimacy continues intact, but Banquo replies with a formality that acknowledges the difference the crown has made:

> Let your highness
> Command upon me, to the which my duties
> Are with a most indissoluble tie
> Forever knit. (3.1.15–18)

As for Macbeth, he has already learned the tyrant's chief lesson: he can have no real friends. His apparently casual question—"Ride you this afternoon?" (3.1.18)—is the prelude to a plot to arrange his friend's murder. "Our fears in Banquo stick deep," broods Macbeth, before giving instructions to the murderers and urging them to be sure to kill Banquo's son, Fleance, as well. For he knows that if Fleance survives, it is possible that the prophecy—that Banquo will beget a royal line—may come true. And if so, Macbeth reflects bitterly, he has defiled his mind and soul only to make "the seeds of Banquo kings!" (3.1.70).

The tyrant's sense of personal defilement is something Shakespeare suggested only at the close of *Richard III*—"I rather hate myself/For hateful deeds committed by myself" (5.3.188–89); it haunts Macbeth from the beginning. And along with this sense that he has fouled his own nest is something he calls "restless ecstasy" (3.2.22)—that is, a constant, all-consuming anxiety. He focuses that anxiety on Banquo, as if he alone stands between himself and happiness: "There is none but he/Whose being I do fear" (3.1.54–55). But the inner torment Macbeth discloses to his wife will not be cured by the murderers he has hired to dispatch his friend.

Lady Macbeth knows that her husband's psychic state threatens them both. "Naught's had, all's spent," she reflects to herself,

> Where our desire is got without content.
> 'Tis safer to be that which we destroy
> Than by destruction dwell in doubtful joy.
> (3.2.4–7)

But what exactly did she expect? Tyranny comes about, as her words acknowledge, through destruction, the destruction of people and of a whole country. That she somehow thought that their personal contentment, safety, and joy could be achieved by this means is in keeping with the fatal shallowness she voiced when she washed the murdered king's blood off her hands: "A little water clears us of this deed" (2.2.70).

The intimate bond between husband and wife was instrumental in their fatal decision to kill Duncan, and in the devastating aftermath of their act, which they carried out together, it is the one human bond that remains for either of them. But nothing that Lady Macbeth now says to her husband—"Why do you keep alone?," "What's done is done," "Be bright and jovial"—quiets the torment within him. Her attempts at forced cheerfulness and reassuring matter-of-factness ring hollow in the face of his anguish: "Oh, full of scorpions is my mind, dear wife!" (3.2.35). For his own part, though he continues to use terms of endearment altogether rare for Shakespeare's married couples, he is no longer sharing his dark designs with her. "What's to be done?" she asks about Banquo, and he replies, "Be innocent of the knowledge, dearest chuck,/Till thou applaud the deed" (3.2.44–45).

Her opportunity to applaud comes that very night, but it all goes horribly wrong. The murderers return to tell Macbeth that they have killed Banquo—"safe in a ditch he bides,/With twenty trenchèd gashes on his head" (3.4.27–28)—but that they have failed to make his son similarly "safe." Macbeth's response reveals a great deal about his particular psychological condition and, more generally, about the fantasies and burdens of tyranny. "Then comes my fit again," he says when he is informed of Fleance's escape;

> I had else been perfect,
> Whole as the marble, founded as the rock,
> As broad and general as the casing air,
> But now I am cabined, cribbed, confined, bound in
> To saucy doubts and fears. (3.4.22–26)

"I had else been perfect"—Macbeth longs to possess a form of completeness, the hardness, solidity, and invulnerability of stone or, alternatively, the pervasiveness, invisibility, and unlimited extension of air. In either case, the dream is to escape from the human condition, which he experiences as unendurably claustrophobic. The longing is almost pitiable; it seems even to harbor an unrealizable spiritual dimension, until one takes in that the means by which Macbeth hopes to become "perfect" is the double murder of his friend and his friend's son.

Here, as throughout Shakespeare, the tyrant's course of behavior is fueled by a pathological narcissism. The lives of others do not matter; what matters is only that he should somehow feel "whole" and "founded." Let the universe fall apart, he has told his wife, let heaven and earth suffer destruction,

> Ere we will eat our meal in fear, and sleep
> In the affliction of these terrible dreams
> That shake us nightly. (3.2.17–19)

No doubt those dreams are truly terrible, and though he has brought them on himself, we might even generate a twinge of sympathy for the nightmares he must endure. But any sympathy is brought up short by his own vicious indifference to anyone and anything else, including the planet itself: "Let the frame of things disjoint" (3.2.16).

It is not enough for the tyrant to destroy a man who represents a moral alternative to the corrupt course he has taken. "'Tis much he dares," he says of Banquo,

> And to that dauntless temper of his mind
> He hath a wisdom that doth guide his valor
> To act in safety. (3.1.5–54)

He must also destroy, if he possibly can, that man's son. Tyranny attempts to poison not merely the present but generations to come, to extend itself forever. It is not the exigencies of plot alone that make Macbeth, like Richard, the killer of children. Tyrants are enemies of the future.

But it proves more difficult to eradicate both future and past than the tyrant imagines. Fleance manages to flee. And just as Richard was haunted in his dream by the ghosts of those he has killed, so Macbeth, at the royal banquet he and his wife host, is haunted by the blood-spattered ghost of Banquo. The apparition figures as an emblem not of the tyrant's repressed conscience but, rather, of his psychological deterioration. Lady Macbeth attempts to stiffen her husband's resolve, as she had earlier done. "Are you a man?" she asks, rebuking him for his weakness:

> Oh, these flaws and starts,
> Impostors to true fear, would well become
> A woman's story at a winter's fire,
> Authorized by her grandam. Shame itself!
>   (3.4.64–67)

But the intimacy that once made her sexual taunting so powerful has eroded, and Macbeth's terror only intensifies. Those who witness his frantic behavior and hear his wild words realize that there is something seriously wrong with him.

The dinner guests face a problem that Shakespeare portrays as recurrent and almost inescapable in tyrannies: observers, particularly those with privileged access, see clearly that the leader is mentally unstable. "His highness is not well" (3.4.53), Ross ventures to say when Macbeth is virtually climbing the walls. But what are they supposed to do? Paradoxically, Lady Macbeth tries to cover up the problem by suggesting that her husband has always been subject to these fits: "My lord is often thus/And hath been from his youth" (3.4.54–55). However disturbing that revelation might be, it is less so than would be the onset of mental illness, for at least it implies that Macbeth's proven competence and stability had long coexisted with such occasional outbursts. It is only when the outbursts threaten to disclose the tyrant's criminal culpability that Lady Macbeth quickly dismisses the assembled company: "At once, good night," she says to them. "Stand not upon the order of your going,/But go at once"

(3.4.120–22). She does not want them to hear another self-incriminating word.

When they are alone together at last, she listens quietly to his continued ranting—"It will have blood, they say; blood will have blood" (3.4.124)—and does not resume either reproaches or reassurances. It is as if something between them has died. He discloses that he has a new object of suspicion, Macduff, who has refused his invitation, and she asks, in a strangely impersonal tone, "Did you send to him, sir?" He responds that he has spies everywhere and that he now intends to visit the Weird Sisters to see if they might tell him more. To this intention his wife says nothing, and he reveals again the tyrant's terrifying narcissism, to which every else must cede: "For mine own good," he declares flatly, "All causes shall give way" (3.4.137–38). Still she says nothing, and, as if he were voicing an interior monologue, he rehearses his grim conviction that there is no going back. "I am in blood/ Stepped in so far, should I wade no more,/Returning were as tedious as go o'er" (3.4.138–40).

"Tedious" is a telling word to use for the nightmare in which Macbeth finds himself. Considerations of morality, political tactics, or basic intelligence have all disappeared, and in their place is a mere calculation of the effort involved. Better not to stop and think but simply to act on impulse: "Strange things I have in head that will to hand,/Which must be acted ere they may be scanned" (3.4.141–42). Only here does Lady Macbeth venture words that recall their former marital intimacy: "You lack the season of all natures, sleep"

(3.4.143). Her husband agrees: "Come, we'll to sleep." It is the last exchange between them in the play.

What lies ahead is the outcome of Macbeth's desperate search for reassurance and security: his credulous desire to believe the ambiguous and deceptive predictions of the Weird Sisters and his unspeakably vicious decision to order the killing of Macduff's wife and children in the wake of that thane's flight to England. Although insecurity, overconfidence, and murderous rage are strange bedfellows, they all coexist in the tyrant's soul. He has servants and associates, but in effect he is alone. Institutional restraints have all failed. The internal and external censors that keep most ordinary mortals, let alone rulers of nations, from sending irrational messages in the middle of the night or acting on every crazed impulse are absent. "From this moment," Macbeth declares, "The very firstlings of my heart shall be/The firstlings of my hand" (4.1.145–46).

The person with whom he had shared his life is no longer part of it. In a famous sleepwalking scene, we see her grappling with her own inner demons, and it is telling that it is not her husband who observes her frantic attempts to clean her hands—"Out, damned spot!" (5.1.31)—but a physician and a waiting gentlewoman. When word is brought to him that his wife is dead, Macbeth, gearing for battle, scarcely reacts: "She should have died hereafter;/There would have been a time for such a word" (5.5.17–18).

What follows is Shakespeare's most mature and considered attempt to understand what it feels like to be a tyrant.

Macbeth is aware that he is loathed by his people and that his very name, as Malcolm puts it, "blisters our tongues" (4.3.12). He has known virtually from the beginning—from before he treacherously killed Duncan—that he is unfit to be king. He bears all the trappings of his exalted station, but they sit awkwardly upon him, only calling attention to his unfitness. "Now does he feel his title," observes one of his subjects, "Hang loose about him, like a giant's robe/Upon a dwarfish thief" (5.2.20–22). He was once focused on his prospects for a long legacy—"Bring forth men-children only," he told his wife—but no more. And that which lies ahead in his own life, even should he manage to defeat his gathering enemies, is grim enough:

> that which should accompany old age,
> As honor, love, obedience, troops of friends,
> I must not look to have, but in their stead
> Curses, not loud but deep, mouth-honor, breath,
> Which the poor heart would fain deny and dare not.
>
> (5.3.24–28)

"Mouth-honor," the empty praise of those who are paid or compelled to praise him, is the reward he can hope to reap from his time in office.

In *Richard III*, Shakespeare imagined the beleaguered tyrant torn between self-love and self-hate. In *Macbeth*, the playwright probes far deeper. What has it all been for, the betrayals, the empty words, the shedding of so much innocent blood? It is difficult to picture the tyrants of our own times having any such moment of truthful reckoning. But Macbeth describes unflinchingly what he has brought upon himself:

> Tomorrow and tomorrow and tomorrow
> Creeps in this petty pace from day to day
> To the last syllable of recorded time,
> And all our yesterdays have lighted fools
> The way to dusty death. Out, out, brief candle.
> Life's but a walking shadow, a poor player
> That struts and frets his hour upon the stage
> And then is heard no more. It is a tale
> Told by an idiot, full of sound and fury,
> Signifying nothing. (5.5.19–28)

It is important to understand that this devastating experience of utter meaninglessness is not, as in some absurdist contemporary drama, the existential condition of humankind. The play insists that it is the fate precisely of the tyrant, and that word—"tyrant"—echoes and reechoes through the close of the play.

After the Weird Sisters' assurance that Macbeth would not be vanquished until Birnam Wood comes to Dunsinane proves to be a mere trick, the despairing tyrant is left finally to encounter Macduff, the man whose wife and children he destroyed. When Macbeth at first declines to fight, his enemy tells him to "live to be the show and gaze o' th' time" (5.7.54). Indeed, the vilest humiliation Macduff can imagine for Macbeth is for him to be put on public display, with a banner advertising the show:

> We'll have thee, as our rarer monsters are,
> Painted upon a pole and underwrit,
> "Here may you see the tyrant." (5.7.55–57)

Though he has "supped full with horrors" and plumbed the depths of despair, Macbeth sees this carnival-like end as unbearably degrading. Friendless, childless, utterly alone, he has nothing to cling to except bare life, and that life, as he has put it bleakly to himself, has fallen into the sere, the yellow leaf. He fights and is killed. Macduff raises the "cursèd head" he has severed and proclaims that tyranny has come to an end. "The time is free" (5.7.85).

Eight

MADNESS IN
GREAT ONES

RICHARD III AND MACBETH are criminals who come
to power by killing the legitimate rulers who stand in their
way. But Shakespeare was also interested in a more insidious
problem, that posed by those who begin as legitimate rulers
and are then drawn by their mental and emotional instability
toward tyrannical behavior. The horrors they inflict on their
subjects and, ultimately, on themselves are the consequences
of psychological degeneration. They may have thoughtful
counselors and friends, people with a healthy instinct for
self-preservation and a concern for their nation. But it is
extremely difficult for such people to counter madness-
induced tyranny, both because it is unanticipated and because
their long-term loyalty and trust have inculcated habits of
obedience.

In the Britain of *King Lear*, though the aged king begins
to act with the unchecked willfulness of a tyrannical child, at

first no one dares to say a word. Having decided to retire—
"To shake all cares and business from our age,/Conferring
them on younger strengths" (*King Lear* 1.1.37–38)—he assem-
bles his court and announces his "fast intent,"—that is, his
fixed decision. He declares that he will divide his kingdom
into three, distributing the parts to his daughters in propor-
tion to their ability to flatter him:

> Tell me, my daughters,
> Since now we will divest us both of rule,
> Interest of territory, cares of state,
> Which of you shall we say doth love us most,
> That we our largest bounty may extend
> Where nature doth with merit challenge?
> (1.1.46–51)

The idea is insane, and yet no one intervenes.

It is possible that the spectators to this grotesque con-
test say nothing because they believe it is merely a formal
ritual, designed to gratify the autocrat's vanity on the occasion of his retirement. After all, one of the highest-ranking
noblemen, the Earl of Gloucester, remarks in the play's first
moments that he has already seen a map with the division
of the kingdom scrupulously plotted out. And at this point
in Lear's long reign, everyone may be accustomed to the
great leader's boundless desire to hear his praises sung. While
inwardly rolling their eyes, they sit around the table and give
him the "mouth-honor" he wants, telling him how blessed

they are to stand in his shadow, how overwhelmed they are by his accomplishments, and how they value him more "than eye-sight, space and liberty" (1.1.54).

But when Lear's youngest daughter, Cordelia, his favorite, refuses to play the nauseating game, it all suddenly becomes deadly serious. Enraged by Cordelia's principled recalcitrance—"I love your majesty/According to my bond," she says, "no more nor less" (1.1.90–91)—Lear disinherits and curses her. Then finally is opposition to Lear's behavior openly expressed, and only by a solitary person, the Earl of Kent. The loyal Kent begins to speak with the requisite ceremonious courtesy, but Lear abruptly cuts him off. Dropping the courtly manner altogether, the earl then voices his objection directly:

> What wouldst thou do, old man?
> Think'st thou that duty shall have dread to speak
> When power to flattery bows?
> To plainness honor's bound
> When majesty falls to folly. Reserve thy state,
> And in thy best consideration check
> This hideous rashness. (1.2.143–49)

There are other responsible adults in the court. Watching the scene unfold are the king's elder daughters, Goneril and Regan, and their husbands, the Dukes of Albany and Cornwall. But none of them or any of the others in attendance seconds the objection or voices even a modest protest. Only Kent dares to say openly what everyone plainly sees: "Lear is mad" (1.1.143). For his frankness, the truth-teller is banished forever from the kingdom, on pain of death. And still no one else speaks out.

Lear's court faces a serious, possibly insuperable problem. In the distant age in which the play is set, roughly in the eighth century B.C.E., Britain does not seem to have any institutions or offices—parliament, privy council, commissioners, high priests—to moderate or dilute royal power. Though the king, surrounded by his family, his loyal thanes, and his servants, may solicit and receive advice, the crucial decision-making power remains his and his alone. When he expresses his wishes, he expects to be obeyed. But the whole system depends on the assumption that he is in his right mind.

Even in systems that have multiple moderating institutions, the chief executive almost always has considerable power. But what happens when that executive is not mentally fit to hold office? What if he begins to make decisions that threaten the well-being and security of the realm? In the case of King Lear, the ruler had probably never been a model of stability or emotional maturity. Discussing his impulsive cursing of his youngest daughter, the king's cynical older daughters, Goneril and Regan, remark that his advancing years are only intensifying qualities that they have long observed in him. "'Tis the infirmity of his age," one notes, "yet he hath ever but slenderly known himself." "The best and soundest of his time," agrees the other, "hath been but rash" (1.1.289–92).

The disinheriting of their sister Cordelia does not threaten Goneril and Regan. On the contrary, since they get to gobble up her share of the kingdom, it is in their immediate interest. They therefore make no attempt to mitigate their father's tyrannical rage. But they know that he may at any moment turn on them as well. They are dealing with both his deep-rooted habits of mind—what they call their father's "long engraffed condition"—and the effects of old age: "Then must we look from his age to receive not alone the imperfections of long engraffed condition, but therewithal the unruly waywardness that infirm and choleric years bring with them" (1.1.292–95). What particularly worries them are his "unconstant starts" (1.1.296)—that is, outbursts such as they have just witnessed in the banishing of Kent. It is extremely dangerous to have a state run by someone who governs by impulse.

Goneril and Regan are very nasty pieces of work, concerned only for themselves. But they grasp that they have a serious problem on their hands, and they quickly take steps at least to protect their own interests, if not those of the realm. Though their father has decided to turn over the actual running of the state to them and their husbands, he has retained a retinue of a hundred armed servants. These the daughters act almost immediately to remove from his control, lest he do something rash. First they cut the number to fifty, then twenty-five; then the downward spiral continues: "What need you five-and-twenty? Ten? Or five?" asks Goneril. Regan: "What need one?" (2.2.442–44). It is ugly, and it is about to get still uglier. But the stripping away of the retainers stems from the recognition that an impulsive narcissist, accustomed to ordering people about, should not have control even of a very small army.

When he first began to act rashly and self-destructively, Cordelia and Kent were the only ones willing to speak out against Lear's tyrannical behavior. Both of them did so out of loyalty to the very person most outraged by their words, a person they lovingly hoped to protect. With their banishment and Lear's abdication, there is nothing to prevent the country from disintegrating. The disintegration was set off by the king's lawless whim, but it is not he—stripped of his power and falling into madness—who will assume the mantle of tyranny. Rather, it is his vicious daughters, who show themselves to be unconstrained by any respect for the rule of law and indifferent to fundamental norms of human decency.

Kent's loyalty to Lear leads him, at the risk of his life, to return in disguise in order to serve his ruined master. But it is too late to avert the disaster that the king has brought upon himself. Kent has been effectively muzzled; Cordelia has been exiled. The only person who can still say openly what everyone perceives has happened is the Fool, a satirical entertainer—the equivalent of a late-night comedian—who is permitted by social convention to articulate what would otherwise be suppressed or punished. "I am better than thou art now," the Fool says to Lear. "I am a fool, thou art nothing" (1.4.161). And in the new regime presided over by Lear's daughters, even this limited form of free speech is impermissible. Goneril makes clear to her father that she will no longer endure the insolence of his "all-licensed fool" (1.4.168), and

Regan is no better. Shivering and miserable, having been driven out into the wild storm along with the mad king, by the middle of the play the Fool disappears forever.

With Lear, unlike Richard III or Coriolanus, we have almost no glimpses into his childhood, where the seeds of his personality disorder may have been sown. We see only a man who has been long accustomed to getting his way in everything and who cannot abide contradiction. In the midst of his madness, sitting in a wretched hovel with a blind man and a beggar for his company, he still has delusions of grandeur: "When I do stare, see how the subject quakes" (4.6.108). But his insanity is shot through with lightning flashes of hard-earned truth. "They flattered me like a dog," he recalls. Everyone fawned upon him, he now grasps, praising him for mature wisdom when he was in fact still only a callow youth. This is the closest we get to the roots of his narcissism: "To say 'Ay' and 'No' to everything I said! 'Ay' and 'No' too was no good divinity" (4.6.97–100).

Nothing in such an upbringing could prepare Lear to grasp reality in his family, in his realm, or even in his own body. He is a father who wrecks his children; he is a leader who cannot distinguish between honest, truthful servants and corrupt scoundrels; he is a ruler who is unable to perceive, let alone address, the needs of his people. In the first part of the play, when Lear is still on the throne, those people are entirely invisible. It is as if the king has never bothered to take in their existence. Looking into a mirror, he has always seen someone larger than life, "every inch a king" (4.6.108).

Hence his horrible surprise when, cold and shaking with fever, he grasps finally that he has been surrounded by flatterers who have constantly lied to him:

> When the rain came to wet me once, and the wind
> to make me chatter, when the thunder would not
> peace at my bidding, there I found 'em, there I smelt
> 'em out. Go to, they are not men o' their words.
> They told me I was everything. 'Tis a lie. I am not
> ague-proof. (4.6.100–105)

"They told me I was everything." It is a moral triumph of some kind for so extreme a solipsist to realize that he is, after all, subject to the same bodily afflictions as everyone else.

But Shakespeare's play looks soberly at the tragic cost of this quite modest realization. Lear insists that he is "more sinned against than sinning," but he cannot be held entirely innocent of the fact that his two older daughters are twisted monsters who seek to kill him. He is certainly not innocent of the disastrous fate of his youngest daughter, whose moral integrity he spurned and whose love he failed to understand. He has evidently failed, as well, to distinguish between the basic decency of Goneril's husband, Albany, and the sadism of Regan's husband, Cornwall, and he has split his kingdom without grasping the high likelihood of violent conflict between the two ruling parties.

It is only when Lear himself wanders out into a wild storm that he takes in the plight of the homeless in the land over which he has ruled for many decades. As the rain beats down on him, the question he asks is a powerful one:

> Poor naked wretches, wheresoe'er you are,
> That bide the pelting of this pitiless storm,
> How shall your houseless heads and unfed sides,
> Your looped and windowed raggedness defend you
> From seasons such as these? (3.4.29–33)

But even as he asks the question, he knows that it is too late for him to do anything to relieve their suffering: "Oh, I have ta'en/Too little care of this!" (3.4.33–34). And what he now thinks—that the rich should expose themselves to what wretches feel so that they may share some of their superfluous wealth with them—hardly constitutes a new economic vision for the country he has ruled.

The monstrous self-absorption that fueled Lear's catastrophic decisions does not vanish because of his exposure to adversity; it remains the organizing principle of perception. When he encounters a homeless beggar, he can only imagine that the man's miseries came about for the same reason as his own: "Didst thou give all to thy daughters, and art come to this?" (3.4.47–48). Certain that the answer must be yes, Lear begins to curse the poor man's ungrateful daughters. And when Kent (in disguise) corrects the mistake—"He hath no daughters, sir"—Lear explodes in rage: "Death, traitor! Nothing could have subdued nature/To such a lowness but his unkind daughters" (3.4.66–68). Lear has lost everything by this point, but he still has the mind of the tyrant who will brook no disagreement: "Death, traitor!"

Nearing the play's end, after Lear has recovered at least partial sanity, acknowledged the folly of his actions, and begged the forgiveness of Cordelia (who has returned to England to fight on his behalf), he continues to have difficulty distancing himself from the self-centeredness that precipitated the disaster in the first place. Taken captive, along with Cordelia, by forces under the command of the ruthless Edmund, Lear emphatically overrules his daughter's request that they be brought to see her sisters: "No, no, no, no" (5.3.8). Why does he not think that they should try at least to beg some mercy? Because he is in the grip of a fantasy—poignant, hopelessly unrealistic, and in its way supremely selfish—that in prison with his youngest daughter he will, after all, obtain what he had originally intended: to set his rest, as he put it, "on her kind nursery" (1.1.121). "We two alone will sing like birds in a cage," he tells Cordelia;

> So we'll live,
> And pray, and sing, and tell old tales, and laugh
> At gilded butterflies, and hear poor rogues
> Talk of court news, and we'll talk with them too—
> Who loses, and who wins; who's in, who's out—
> And take upon 's the mystery of things,
> As if we were God's spies. (5.3.9–17)

Even were this a fantasy that Cordelia could possibly share and find appealing, she is too realistic to think it is remotely possible. Led away to prison and to the almost certain death that she knows looms there, she is conspicuously, painfully silent.

IN *THE WINTER'S TALE,* a play he wrote late in his career, Shakespeare returned to the idea of a legitimate ruler who, descending into madness, begins to behave like a tyrant. In the case of Leontes, king of Sicilia, the precipitating cause is not senile rage; rather, it is a sudden onset of paranoia, which takes the form of a conviction that his wife, Hermione, then nearing the full term of a pregnancy, has had an adulterous affair and is carrying a child that is not his. His suspicion falls on his best friend, Polixenes, the king of Bohemia, who has been visiting Sicilia for the past nine months. Leontes initially broaches his conviction to his chief counselor, Camillo, who, horrified, tries to disabuse the king of his fixed idea: "Good my lord, be cured/Of this diseased opinion," he urges, and quickly, "For 'tis most dangerous" (*The Winter's Tale* 1.2.296–98). Leontes insists that his charge is true and, when the counselor again demurs, explodes with rage: "It is. You lie, you lie./I say thou liest, Camillo, and I hate thee" (1.2.299–300). The jealous king offers no proof; only his emphatic insistence.

A tyrant does not need to traffic in facts or supply evidence. He expects his accusation to be enough. If he says that someone has been betraying him, or laughing at him, or spying on him, it must be the case. Anyone who contradicts him is either a liar or an idiot. The last thing the tyrant wants, even when he appears to solicit it, is an independent opinion. What he actually wants is loyalty, and by loyalty he does not mean integrity, honor, or responsibility. He means an immediate, unreserved confirmation of his own views and a willingness to carry out his orders without hesitation. When an autocratic, paranoid, narcissistic ruler sits down with a civil servant and asks for his loyalty, the state is in danger.

Hence when Camillo fails to echo Leontes's lunatic suspicion, Leontes bitterly charges him with dishonesty, cowardice, or negligence. And it is not enough to berate him as "a gross lout, a mindless slave,/Or else a hovering temporizer" (1.2.301–2); the king demands that his counselor act to demonstrate absolute loyalty. There is, as Leontes has conceived it, a perfect way to do so. He orders Camillo to poison Polixenes.

Now the counselor is in deep trouble, and he knows it. His royal master is not only mad but also extremely dangerous. Honest attempts to dissuade him have only called forth more rage, and Camillo is aware that if he refuses to act on the king's behest, he will himself be killed. He briefly considers carrying out the order: "To do this deed," he reflects, "Promotion follows." Camillo is a decent human being, not a time-serving villain; this is why he dared to challenge the king in the first place. At the same time, he has no interest in being a martyr. He has therefore only a single option: he warns Polixenes, and at night the two of them, along with the attendants who have accompanied the Bohemian king on his state visit, precipitately flee from Sicilia.

Flight is a desperate option, one from which there is no

looking back, and it is by no means accessible to everyone. As the king's principal counselor, Camillo has the authority to command that the city gates be opened, and Polixenes's ships are already waiting for him in the harbor. Camillo has presumably abandoned all his possessions, along with the high place of trust he has long held, but he evidently has no family to worry about, and the ruler whose life he has just saved will protect and support him. The important thing, in this moment of extremity, is to "take the urgent hour," as Camillo puts it, and get out of the tyrant's range.

But it is not possible for poor Hermione to do so; nor, until he erupts, does she have any inkling that her husband has been eyeing her with increasing suspicion and anger. Awaiting the impending ordeal of childbirth, she has been taking care of her young son, Mamillius, gossiping with her friend Paulina, and serving as the gracious hostess to her husband's best friend. It is indeed Leontes who has urged her to help him induce Polixenes to agree to extend his already long stay in Sicilia. But all of her sweet gestures to that effect have been interpreted by the paranoid Leontes as proofs of her infidelity. "Is whispering nothing?" he fumes, when Camillo attempts to counter his fears.

> Is leaning cheek to cheek? Is meeting noses?
> Kissing with inside lip? Stopping the career
> Of laughter with a sigh—a note infallible
> Of breaking honesty? Horsing foot on foot?
> Skulking in corners? (1.2.284–89)

How much of this is actually true does not matter; it is what Leontes thinks he has seen, and that is sufficient to convict her in his mind.

The flight of Polixenes and Camillo confirms this conviction and intensifies Leontes's sense that he has been made a fool of. It seems abundantly clear to him now that Camillo, whom he had trusted, was Polixenes's co-conspirator, "his pander." There is, he concludes, "a plot against my life," and he moves to counter it by ordering the arrest and imprisonment of his wife: "She's an adulteress," he tells the shocked court. At first his courtiers attempt, as Camillo had done, to dispute the charge and to blame it on a villainous slanderer, "some putter-on/That will be damned for't" (2.1.142–43). "Beseech your highness," one urges. "Call the Queen again." "Be certain what you do, sir," warns another, "lest your justice/Prove violence" (2.1.127–29).

Leontes will not listen. "You smell this business," he tells them, "with a sense as cold/As is a dead man's nose" (2.1.152–53). He is not interested in hearing what they have observed and does not require their approval. "What need we/Commune with you of this," he asks dismissively, "but rather follow/Our forceful instigation?" (2.1.162–64). To follow his instigation means to go with his impulse and his alone:

> We need no more of your advice. The matter—
> The loss, the gain, the ordering on't—
> Is all properly ours. (2.1.169–71)

Of course, from the perspective of the court, the "matter"—an accusation of a plot against the life of the ruler, the flight of the king's principal counselor, and the imprisonment of the queen—is hardly Leontes's alone. But in the manner characteristic of tyrants, he has folded the whole state into himself. The one concession he has made—a concession, as he puts it, "to th' minds of others"—is to send ambassadors to "Sacred Delphos, to Apollo's temple," to consult the oracle. The courtiers, otherwise silenced, approve.

As in *King Lear* a woman—the autocrat's youngest daughter—takes the decisive, public step of refusing her father's peremptory demand, so, too, in *The Winter's Tale* it is a woman who most strongly opposes the tyrant's will. The principal challenger is not Leontes's wronged wife, Hermione—though she defends herself courageously and eloquently—but Hermione's friend Paulina. It is she who visits the imprisoned queen and proposes, in the hopes of returning the king to his senses, to present to him the baby the queen has newly delivered. When the jailor worries, perfectly reasonably, that he may run a risk if he allows the baby to be removed from the prison without a warrant, Paulina eloquently reassures him:

> You need not fear it, sir.
> This child was prisoner to the womb and is
> By law and process of great nature thence
> Freed and enfranchised, not a party to
> The anger of the King, nor guilty of—
> If any be—the trespass of the Queen. (2.2.59–64)

For a brief, telling moment we glimpse the bureaucratic structure that characterizes all regimes and that becomes particularly important when the leader is behaving in alarming ways. If there is a procedural anomaly, a high-ranking person—and Paulina, the aristocratic wife of the king's counselor Antigonus, is of very high rank indeed—needs to step forward and take responsibility. "Do not you fear," she again tells the jailor; "I/Will stand betwixt you and danger" (2.2.66–67).

There is, we immediately learn, good reason to fear. The tyrant is unable to sleep: "Nor night, nor day, no rest" (2.3.1). His son, Mamillius, has fallen ill, in the wake of the charges brought against Hermione, and in addition to worrying about the boy, Leontes has been brooding constantly on revenge. Polixenes and Camillo are beyond his reach— "plot-proof," as he puts it—but "th' adulteress" is within his power (2.3.4–6). "Say that she were gone,/Given to the fire" (2.3.7–8), he muses darkly, then he might recover at least some of his ability to sleep.

Small wonder that when Paulina arrives carrying the baby, the lords who attend on Leontes tell her that she cannot enter. But far from leaving quietly, she appeals to them to help her. "Fear you his tyrannous passion," she asks, "more, alas,/Than the Queen's life?" (2.3.27–28). They explain that he has not been able to sleep, but she counters, "I come to bring him sleep" and blames them, in effect, for heightening his insanity:

Tis such as you,
That creep like shadows by him and do sigh
At each his needless heavings—such as you
Nourish the cause of his awaking. (2.3.33–36)

Hers is a wildly audacious strategy—to try to snap the
king out of his madness by forcing him to take up a child he
fervently believes is not his—and it fails. Leontes's rage only
intensifies. He orders that the "bastard" be burned and then
turns on Paulina and threatens to have her burned as well.
"I care not," the intrepid woman replies, adding some of the
most magnificent words of defiance in all of Shakespeare:

It is an heretic that makes the fire,
Not she which burns in't. (2.3.114–15)

It is the effect of tyranny to invert the whole structure of
authority: legitimacy no longer resides at the center of the
state; instead, it is vested in the victims of its violence.

Paulina has already referred to the king's "tyrannous
passion," and she has said flatly, to his face, "you are mad."
But it is a sign of the gravity of the direct charge of tyranny
that she slightly holds back. "I'll not call you tyrant," she
tells him,

But this most cruel usage of your queen—
Not able to produce more accusation

> Than your own weak-hinged fancy—something
> savors
> Of tyranny. (2.3.115–18)

For his part, Leontes does not let these words pass unchallenged. "Were I a tyrant," he tells the courtiers, "Where were her life? She durst not call me so,/If she did know me one" (2.3.121–23). Perhaps Paulina's words were strategic: given his response, Leontes is scarcely in a position to follow up on his order that she be burned. He simply orders her out of the room.

Paulina's life is spared, but Leontes's madness and his tyrannical impulses are unchecked. Suspecting that her husband, Antigonus, has contrived to have Paulina bring the baby to him, he accuses the counselor of treason. To demonstrate that he is not a traitor, Antigonus must kill the infant. "Take it up straight," Leontes commands him.

> Within this hour bring me word 'tis done,
> And by good testimony, or I'll seize thy life
> With what thou else call'st thine. (2.3.134–37)

There is no legal process; no respect for civilized norms; no decency. In a society where suspicion and certainty are indistinguishable, loyalty is proved by carrying out the tyrant's murderous commands.

There remains, however, some moral strength in Sicilia. Leontes's tyranny is the result of a sudden, inexplicable descent into madness; until very recently he has been not a clownish thug but a respected, entirely legitimate ruler. Hence, as Camillo and Paulina have both demonstrated, he is surrounded not by timeservers but by decent people who have been accustomed to speaking their minds. And though his court is shocked and terrified—"You're liars all" (2.3.145), Leontes rages at them—they are not completely silenced, even now. "We have always truly served you, and beseech/So to esteem of us" (2.3.147–48), says one of the courtiers, kneeling down and pleading with the king to change his horrible command to have the newborn child burned to death. Leontes reluctantly agrees, but only to the extent of ordering Antigonus to take the infant to some remote place and expose it to the elements.

In the tangled romance plot that then unfolds, this changed command has important consequences. It leads to the death of Antigonus (via the notorious stage direction "Exit, pursued by a bear" [3.3.57]) and eventually to the near-miraculous recovery, sixteen years later, of Leontes's daughter, Perdita. But at the moment that, in response to the court's pleading, Leontes slightly modifies his order to kill the infant, very little has changed in his behavior or intention. That is part of the point: once the state is in the hands of an unstable, impulsive, and vindictive tyrant, there is almost nothing that the ordinary mechanisms of moderation can accomplish. Sensible advice falls on deaf ears; dignified demurrals are brushed aside; outspoken protests only seem to make matters worse.

Determined to avenge himself on the wife he believes has betrayed him, Leontes puts Hermione on trial for high treason. "Let us be cleared/Of being tyrannous," he declares, as he calls for the prisoner to appear, "since we so openly/ Proceed in justice" (3.2.4–6). The open proceeding may seem preferable, from a public relations standpoint, to the poison with which he intended to dispatch his best friend, but everyone in Shakespeare's world knew perfectly well that there was only one possible outcome. The ruler controlled the institutions that conferred the stamp of reality upon even his wildest claims. This is a show trial, in the manner of Henry VIII or, in our own time, Stalin.

There is, however, one small but significant difference: in *The Winter's Tale,* the person accused of treason is not so broken in spirit as to confess to the imaginary crime. On the contrary, with dignity and steely grace she exposes the tyrant's "justice" for what it is:

> Since what I am to say must be but that
> Which contradicts my accusation, and
> The testimony on my part no other
> But what comes from myself, it shall scarce boot me
> To say, "Not guilty." (3.2.20–24)

All the same, she professes her faith that "if powers divine/ Behold our human actions—as they do," then her "innocence shall make/False accusation blush and tyranny/Tremble at patience" (3.2.26–30).

What would it mean for tyranny to tremble at patience? There are forms of resistance whose power resides not in striking back against unjust blows—something that Hermi-

one, in any case, is in no position to do—but in enduring
and waiting, waiting both for personal vindication and for
the oppressor's possible moral awakening. In the grip of his
delusion and self-righteous indignation, Leontes cannot perceive this power, let alone tremble at it. As he continues to
bring charges against his wife, one more fantastical than the
last, Hermione ceases even to attempt to make sense of them:
"You speak a language that I understand not" (3.2.78), she says.
"My life stands in the level"—that is, as the target—"of your
dreams" (3.2.79). Leontes's response inadvertently gets at the
heart of the problem: "Your actions are my dreams" (3.2.80).
If the tyrant dreams that there is fraud, or betrayal, or treason,
then there is fraud, or betrayal, or treason.

It is, in consequence, almost impossible to break through
the solipsistic, self-justifying fantasies. The ambassadors
return from Apollo's temple bearing the sealed oracle, which
has, when opened and read out in the courtroom, none of the
ambiguity in which such messages usually trafficked:

> "Hermione is chaste, Polixenes blameless, Camillo
> a true subject, Leontes a jealous tyrant, his inno-
> cent babe truly begotten; and the King shall live
> without an heir if that which is lost be not found."
> (3.2.130–33)

But even now, there is no relief from the jealous tyrant's fixed
idea. "There is no truth at all i' th' oracle," he stubbornly
declares and then orders the trial to proceed.

It is only when word is brought that his son, Mamillius, has died from sheer anguish over and fear at his mother's fate that Leontes finally receives a shock severe enough to snap him out of his madness. Taking his son's death as a dreadful sign of Apollo's anger at his injustice, he wishes to act at once to rectify at least some of the damage he has done: "I'll reconcile me to Polixenes,/New woo my queen, recall the good Camillo" (3.4.152–53). But it is not so easy. Hermione has collapsed at the news of her son's death, and now the distraught Paulina enters with bitter words. Earlier, she had struggled to temper her sharp tongue: "I'll not call you tyrant." Now, dropping all vestige of restraint, she bitterly asks Leontes, "What studied torments, tyrant, hast for me?" (3.2.172). His tyranny and his jealousies together, she tells him, have not merely tempted him to try to corrupt Camillo into murdering Polixenes, and not merely induced him to cast his infant daughter to the crows, and not merely led to the death of his son. Now, as their masterpiece, they have caused the death of his wife.

The court is horrified by Paulina's brutal frankness. But the trauma has made Leontes a different ruler and a different man. He welcomes the truth and acknowledges the terrible destruction he has caused. The play does not depict him driven from his throne and wandering as a homeless wretch, like Lear, through his former kingdom. He continues as the king of Sicilia, but he embarks on a long exercise of remorse and self-reproach. It is only after sixteen years have elapsed—Father Time makes an appearance and urges the audience to think that it has somehow slept through this extended interval—that the story resumes.

When it does so, Leontes is still in the midst of the deepest penance. His courtiers urge him finally to forgive himself, remarry, and give the kingdom an heir to the throne. But Paulina, who serves, in effect, as his therapist, is unrelenting in forcing him to face what he has done and to remain unmarried. "If one by one you wedded all the world," she tells him,

> Or from the all that are took something good
> To make a perfect woman, she you killed
> Would be unparalleled. (5.1.13–16)

"Killed?/She I killed?" Leontes replies. "I did so," he acknowledges, "but thou strik'st me/Sorely to say I did" (5.1.16–18). He agrees never to remarry without Paulina's consent.

In the end, *The Winter's Tale* contrives to reunite the king with his lost daughter and, through a spectacular theatrical coup, with the wife he had believed dead. In the hushed space of Paulina's gallery, Leontes comes to view what he is told is a statue of Hermione. Seemingly miraculously, the statue comes to life, steps down from the pedestal, and embraces her husband and her daughter. But nothing can fully erase the memory of tyranny, nothing can bring back the sixteen years spent in isolation and misery, nothing can restore the sweet innocence of friendship, trust, and love. When Leontes is astonished to see his wife again, he is at first struck by the signs of her aging: "Hermione was not so much wrinkled, nothing/So aged as this seems" (5.3.28–29). New life may lie on the other side of years lost to tyranny, but this life will not be the same as it once was. The most poignant emblem in the play for all that tyranny makes unrecoverable is the little boy Mamillius, who died of grief and who is not magically resurrected in the giddy succession of happy reunions.

Still, more than any of Shakespeare's other plays, *The Winter's Tale* allows itself the dream of a second chance. The event that makes this renewal possible, in the wake of disaster, is one of the playwright's most daring and implausible fantasies: the tyrant's full, unfeigned, utterly sincere repentance. Imagining this inner transformation is almost as difficult as imagining a statue coming to life.

Nine

DOWNFALL AND
RESURGENCE

THE HAPPY ENDING in *The Winter's Tale* is in keeping
with the literary genre of romance, with its deliberate, play-
ful violation of realistic expectations. Shakespeare and his
audience knew perfectly well that the historical record rarely
features the miraculous redemption of unstable tyrannical
rulers. Escape from that somber knowledge was part of the
lure of this genre, with its wild plot twists and its culminating
cascade of wondrous reunion, reconciliation, and forgiveness. "Such a deal of wonder is broken out within this hour,"
remarks one observer at the play's end, "that ballad-makers
cannot be able to express it" (*Winter's Tale* 5.2.21–23).

But Shakespeare did not solely indulge in fantasy solu-
tions to the dilemmas tyranny posed. On the contrary, *The
Winter's Tale* is a rare release from the realistic thinking that
occupied him for much of his career, thinking that returned
to the ways in which the nightmare could be brought to an

end. The tyrant, the playwright reflected, always and neces-
sarily has powerful enemies. He can hunt down and murder
some of them; he can compel others to bend under his will
and to offer him what Macbeth calls "mouth-honor." He can
employ spies in every house and listen in the dark to whatever
is being whispered around him. He can reward his followers, rally his troops, and stage an endless succession of public
events that celebrate his innumerable accomplishments. But
he cannot possibly eliminate everyone who hates him. For
eventually almost everyone does.

No matter how tight a net the tyrant weaves, someone
always manages to slip through and make it to safety. "Thou
must not stay," says the Roman general Titus Andronicus
to Lucius, the only survivor of his twenty-five sons. The
tyrant Saturninus has just slaughtered his son's two remaining brothers and countenanced the rape and mutilation of his
sister. Lucius escapes to the Goths, where he raises an army
and returns to kill the tyrant and assume power. "May I govern so," he declares in the end, "To heal Rome's harms and
wipe away her woe" (*Titus Andronicus* 5.3.145–46). Similarly,
in *Richard III* Queen Elizabeth urges her son Dorset to "go,
cross the seas/And live with Richmond" in Brittany. "Go,"
she pleads, "hie thee, hie thee, from this slaughterhouse"
(*Richard III* 4.1.41–43). His brother, his uncle, and his two
half brothers have been killed by the tyrant, along with innumerable others, but Dorset succeeds in joining Richmond,
who leads the forces that topple the hated tyrant. The victor,
making a similar pledge at the play's end to heal the nation's

wounds, offers a prayer: "God, if Thy will be so,/Enrich the time to come with smooth-faced peace/With smiling plenty, and fair prosperous days" (5.5.32–34).

So, too, in *Macbeth* the murdered king's sons realize the imminent danger they are in. This is hardly the moment to offer ceremonious thanks to their hosts, the Macbeths. "What should be spoken here," one whispers to the other, "where our fate,/Hid in an auger-hole, may rush and seize us?" "Therefore, to horse," agrees the other. "And let us not be dainty of leave-taking" (*Macbeth* 2.3.118–19, 140–41). The sons sneak off, endure the false charge that they were parricides, and live to bring down the tyrant. The play, however, ends on a darker note than either *Titus* or *Richard III*. Malcolm, the newly proclaimed king of Scotland, says that he plans not only to call home "our exiled friends abroad/ That fled the snares of watchful tyranny" but also to produce forth, presumably for trial, "the cruel ministers/Of this dead butcher and his fiend-like queen" (5.7.96–99). There will be a reckoning.

Slip away, get out of the tyrant's range, make your way across a border, join forces with other exiles, and return with an invasion force. That is the basic strategy, and it is not only a literary one: it has served for resistance fighters in Nazi Germany, Vichy France, and many others places. As Shakespeare understood, the strategy is hardly without risk. The plan may go awry, as Buckingham's does, and end in execution rather than escape. Friends and family may suffer. The tyrant may hold a loved one hostage, as when Richard III seizes Lord Stanley's son in order to ensure his loyalty: "Look your heart be firm," he tells the anguished father. "Or else his head's assurance is but frail" (*Richard III* 4.4.495–96). As Macduff finds, the blow may fall heavily on innocent loved ones left behind.

The high cost of this resistance strategy is most powerfully depicted in *King Lear*. Though her father had in senile rage disinherited her before his retirement, Cordelia is determined to save him from her two evil older sisters, Goneril and Regan, who, with their husbands, rule the country and who now seek the old man's life. Returning to Britain from France, whose king she had wed, and leading a French army, she declares the altruism of her motives: "No blown ambition doth our arms incite,/But love, dear love, and our aged father's right" (*King Lear* 4.3.25–26). Her forces have secretly been in contact with important figures in the kingdom, people who have been shocked by the harsh treatment of the old king by Goneril and Regan and who have taken note of the tension between their husbands, the well-meaning but weak Duke of Albany and the unspeakably cruel Duke of Cornwall. The stage seems set for the restoration of decency, a victory comparable to that of Richmond over Richard or Malcolm over Macbeth.

But it does not happen. Instead, against all expectations, the forces of the wicked sisters triumph. Cordelia and her army are defeated. Taken captive, she and her father are sent to prison, and Edmund, the general who has led the victorious British forces, secretly orders her murder. Since

Albany is ineffectual and Regan's husband, Cornwall, has died, Edmund is poised to take over the realm. The bastard son of the Earl of Gloucester, he has no legitimate claim to the throne. But he sums up in his person many of the tyrant's attributes. He is bold, inventive, conniving, hypocritical, and utterly ruthless. He has reached his position first by hatching a plot that led to his brother Edgar's banishment and then by betraying his own father. Both wicked sisters are mad for him, and he muses jauntily over his choice: "Which of them shall I take?/Both? One? Or neither?" (5.1.47–48).

In all of the historical sources, the virtuous Cordelia is the victor and assumes the throne, but in Shakespeare's version, Cordelia, shockingly, is hanged in prison. She has been the embodiment in the play of everything decent and upright, the hope of redemption from all the cruelty and injustice that have been visited upon the kingdom. Her death leaves a wound that will never completely heal. But at least the triumph of evil is short-lived. Regan is poisoned by her jealous sister, Goneril; Edmund is killed in single combat by his brother, Edgar, against whom he had wickedly plotted; and Goneril commits suicide. At the end, none of the truly vicious people in the play is alive to enjoy the fruits of victory.

Still, their deaths cannot not erase the tragedy of Cordelia's loss or the unspeakable grief of her father, who dies heartbroken by what has transpired:

> And my poor fool is hanged. No, no, no life?
> Why should a dog, a horse, a rat have life,

And thou no breath at all? Thou'lt come no more,
Never, never, never, never, never! (5.3.281–84)

Shakespeare insists here, more poignantly and urgently than anywhere else in his work, on the irreparability of the losses that tyranny leaves in its wake. There is no equivalent to Richmond's proud declaration in *Richard III* "The day is ours; the bloody dog is dead" (*Richard III* 5.5.2) or to Macduff's "Behold where stands/Th'usurper's cursèd head. The time is free" (*Macbeth* 5.7.84–85). When in *King Lear* a messenger announces, "Edmund is dead, my lord," Albany replies, "That's but a trifle here" (*King Lear* 5.3.271).

Shakespeare did not think that tyrants ever lasted for very long. However cunning they were in their rise, once in power they were surprisingly incompetent. Possessing no vision for the country they ruled, they were incapable of fashioning enduring support, and though they were cruel and violent, they could never crush all of the opposition. Their isolation, suspicion, and anger, often conjoined to an arrogant overconfidence, hastened their downfall. The plays that depict tyranny inevitably end at least with gestures toward the renewal of community and the restoration of legitimate order.

But in *King Lear*, the overwhelming emphasis on what is called the "general woe" and the "gored state" makes it difficult for Shakespeare to stage these gestures. The most plausible candidate to pick up the broken pieces is the young Edgar. The last lines in the play are in one early text given to him; in another, to Albany, who is decently inclined but morally compromised. It seems as if the actors in the company were competing to deliver them or as if Shakespeare himself was uncertain. In any case, the lines are not, as we might have expected them to be, a manifestation of political leadership. They are, rather, the expression of the traumatic aftermath of the kingdom's ordeal:

> The weight of this sad time we must obey;
> Speak what we feel, not what we ought to say.
> The oldest hath borne most; we that are young
> Shall never see so much, nor live so long.
>
> (5.3.299–302)

This is the voice of a man speaking for a community in a state of shock.

In *Richard III*, the main opposition to tyranny forms around the Earl of Richmond; in *Macbeth*, around the king's son Malcolm. Both assume power at the end. There is no comparable figure in *King Lear*. Instead—and astonishingly—the moral courage is glimpsed in a very minor character far below the society's social radar and whose name we never learn. It is a servant, one of the mass of domestics who surround all figures of great wealth and authority, and he does not like what he is seeing. His master, Regan's husband, the Duke of Cornwall, is personally conducting an interrogation. In the wake of Lear's retirement, Cornwall is one of the two rulers of the country, and he has got word of the French inva-

sion force led by Cordelia with the aim of restoring Lear to
the throne. It is imperative to keep the old king from reaching Cordelia's army, but Cornwall has now learned that the
nobleman whose house he is in, the elderly Earl of Gloucester,
is collaborating with the invaders and has sent Lear to Dover.

Cornwall has Gloucester bound to a chair and, together
with his wife, begins to question him roughly: "Wherefore to
Dover? . . . Wherefore to Dover? . . . Wherefore to Dover?"
(3.7.50–55). Failing to get the answers he wants and increasingly enraged, Cornwall tells his servants to hold the chair.
He then leans over and tears out one of Gloucester's eyes.
The scene is startling—members of the theater audience often
faint—but what immediately follows might have seemed to a
Renaissance audience, who knew that suspected traitors were
often tortured, even more startling. As the fiendish Regan
urges her husband to pluck out the other eye too, a voice suddenly calls out, "Hold your hand, my lord" (3.7.72). Shakespeare does nothing to soften the shock of the unexpected
command. The words are spoken not by one of Gloucester's
sons, by a noble bystander, by a gentleman in disguise, or even
by someone in Gloucester's household. They are spoken by
one of Cornwall's own servants, someone long accustomed
simply to doing his bidding. "I have served you ever since
I was a child," he declares. "But better service have I never
done you/Than now to bid you hold" (3.7.73–75).

King Lear does not address the subject of tyranny in any
theoretical way. But it stages unforgettably a moment when
someone in the ruler's service feels compelled to stop what he

is witnessing. Regan is outraged at the interruption: "How now, you dog?" (3.7.75). And Cornwall, drawing his sword and using the term for feudal vassal, is no less so: "My villein?" (3.7.78). There follows a violent skirmish, master against servant, that ends when Regan, astonished that a menial would dare anything of the kind—"A peasant stand up thus?"—runs him through and kills him.

The scene of torture then continues, as Cornwall gouges out Gloucester's remaining eye. The loathsome husband and wife drive the blinded man out of his own house with one of the cruelest commands in all of Shakespeare—"Go, thrust him out at gates, and let him smell/His way to Dover" (3.7.94–95)—and Cornwall disposes of the corpse of the servant who presumed to attempt to restrain him: "Throw this slave/Upon the dunghill" (3.7.97–98). But it turns out that the servant's death was not in vain. Cornwall has received a wound from which he shortly after dies. His death, along with the public revulsion aroused by the sight of the blinded old man, significantly weakens the party of Goneril, Regan, and Edmund.

Shakespeare did not believe that the common people could be counted upon as a bulwark against tyranny. They were, he thought, too easily manipulated by slogans, cowed by threats, or bribed by trivial gifts to serve as reliable defenders of freedom. His tyrannicides are drawn, for the most part, from the same elite whose members generate the unjust rulers they oppose and eventually kill. In *King Lear*'s nameless servant, however, he created a figure who serves as the very essence of popular resistance to tyrants. That man refuses to remain silent and watch. It costs him his life, but he stands up for human decency. Though he is a very minor figure with only a handful of lines, he is one of Shakespeare's great heroes.

THE DEVASTATION AT the close of *Lear* poses in its most extreme form questions that hover over all of Shakespeare's representations of tyranny: How can alert and courageous people not merely escape from the tyrant's grasp, in order to fight against him and try to topple him, but prevent him from coming to power in the first place? How is it possible to stop the devastation from happening? In *Richard III*, the hate-crazed Queen Margaret, hovering around the court of King Edward like a dark nemesis, tries to warn the Duke of Buckingham, whom she exempts from her hatred, to beware of Richard:

> Take heed of yonder dog.
> Look when he fawns, he bites; and when he bites,
> His venom tooth will rankle to the death.
> Have not to do with him, beware of him;
> Sin, death, and hell have set their marks on him,
> And all their ministers attend on him.
> (*Richard III* 1.3.288–93)

But the duke dismisses her warning and serves instead as one of the prime enablers in Richard's rise to power—until he himself falls beneath Richard's axe.

In *Lear,* the courageous Earl of Kent speaks out boldly to try to persuade the king he loyally serves to stop his madness and withdraw the curse he has bestowed on the only daughter who actually loves him. But, in the face of Lear's rage, no one takes Kent's side, and he is banished on pain of death. When Kent disguises himself in order to continue to serve his master, he is entirely unable to stop the catastrophic decline. If anything, his belligerent boldness only further whets the anger of the two wicked daughters, and the kingdom, like the old king himself, spirals into madness and disaster.

There is one play in Shakespeare's whole career that features a systematic, principled attempt to stop tyranny before it starts. *Julius Caesar* opens with the tribunes Murellus and Flavius angrily trying to stop the commoners from celebrating Caesar's triumph over Pompey. They see clearly that the mob's excitement around the general has dangerous political ramifications, and they rush to pull down the decorations that have been hung on his statues:

> These growing feathers plucked from Caesar's wing
> Will make him fly an ordinary pitch,
> Who else would soar above the view of men
> And keep us all in servile fearfulness.
> (*Julius Caesar* 1.1.71–74)

Their efforts are not without risk. "Murellus and Flavius," we are told, "for pulling scarves off Caesar's images, are put to silence" (1.2.278–79).

In the play's second scene, two key figures in Rome's sena-
torial elite share with each other the same anxiety. Conversing with Cassius, Brutus starts every time he hears the roar of
the crowd in the distance. "What means this shouting?" he
asks nervously. "I do fear the people/Choose Caesar for their
king" (1.2.79–80). Cassius seizes on the opportunity to express
his own anger and perplexity at Caesar's exalted position:

> Why, man, he doth bestride the narrow world
> Like a Colossus, and we petty men
> Walk under his huge legs and peep about
> To find ourselves dishonorable graves. (1.2.135–38)

The key thing, Cassius urges, is to understand that what
is happening is not some mysterious, ineluctable fate. "The
fault, dear Brutus, is not in our stars,/But in ourselves, that
we are underlings" (1.2.140–41). And this means, by implication, that it is possible to do something about the imminent
threat of tyranny.

Brutus is himself highly alert to this implication and has
given it much thought on his own. He promises Cassius to
continue the conversation in the near future. Before they
part, they learn that the shouts of the crowd came when Caesar thrice refused the crown that Antony offered him. This
refusal hardly settles the matter. Casca reports a rumor about
what the Senate plans to do the next day: to make Caesar a
king who can wear his crown everywhere but in Italy. Cassius
responds by claiming that he would rather commit suicide

than live under such domination. The ability to end one's own life, he suggests, confers a kind of freedom: "Therein, ye gods, you make the weak most strong;/Therein, ye gods, you tyrants do defeat" (1.3.91–92).

Brutus, as we shortly learn, is also thinking about freedom from tyranny, but his thoughts do not turn to suicide. "It must be by his death" (2.1.10), he says. His words are not part of a conversation. They are not even overheard by anyone on the stage: he has conspicuously dismissed his servant. In his orchard in the middle of the night, he is brooding by himself. Neither the "It" in "It must be" nor the "his" in "his death" are specified. We are plunged into a mind in motion, and thus there is no prologue.

> It must be by his death; and for my part
> I know no personal cause to spurn at him
> But for the general. He would be crowned:
> How that might change his nature, there's the
>   question.
> It is the bright day that brings forth the adder,
> And that craves wary walking. Crown him that.
>   (2.1.10–15)

Shakespeare had never written anything like this. What are we supposed to make of it?

Brutus invokes "the general"—that is, the common good—as opposed to a "personal cause," but his long soliloquy undermines any attempt to draw a clean line between abstract political principles and particular individuals, with their psychological peculiarities, their unpredictability, their only partially knowable, opaque inwardness. The verbs "would" and "might" shimmer and dance their ambiguous way through the twists and turns of a mind obsessed. The resonant phrase "there's the question," which anticipates Hamlet's famous words, extends like a miasma across the whole of Brutus's train of thought.

Ancient Romans liked to think of themselves as the great figures not of self-reflection but of action. They would conquer the world and leave philosophical investigations and neurotic navel-gazing to the Greeks. For Shakespeare, however, behind the screen of public rhetoric in Rome there were troubled, vulnerable, conflicted people uncertain of the right course to take and only half aware of what was driving them to act. The danger was all the greater because they were acting on a world stage, and their obscure private motives had massive, potentially catastrophic public consequences.

"There's the question," Brutus says, not quite saying what the question is. Tangled together, several different questions are tormenting him. In how much danger is the Roman republic, which I love and will defend with my life? What does Cassius want from me? How likely is it that Caesar—who has just thrice refused a proffered crown—will develop into a tyrant? What is the best way to prevent a disaster? How should my close, long-term personal friendship with Caesar factor into whatever decision I reach? Would it make more sense simply to watch and wait?

A piece of proverbial folk wisdom—"It is the bright day

that brings forth the adder"—gives way to a cautionary warning: "And that craves wary walking." Both then yield to an incoherent, ungrammatical exclamation—"Crown him that"—that seems the verbal trace of a fantasy passing unbidden through Brutus's mind. So the speech continues, twisting together the natural with the social, mingling both eyewitness observation and personal fantasy, driving incoherently and fatefully toward an assassination plot whose public justification is a kind of press release the killer is already fashioning:

> And since the quarrel
> Will bear no color for the thing he is,
> Fashion it thus: that what he is, augmented,
> Would run to these and these extremities.
> (2.1.28–31)

We are witnessing the genealogy of one of the great world-historical events, the assassination of Julius Caesar, but we are asked to view it both from without and within.

The characters in *Julius Caesar* attempt to define themselves in relation to distinct political and philosophical principles. Cassius claims that he is a follower of Epicurus, which implies that he believes that humans alone, and not the gods or fate, are responsible for their own happiness or unhappiness. Cicero maintains, as the academic school of skeptical philosophers did, that "men may construe things after their fashion,/Clean from the purpose of the things themselves" (1.3.34–35). Brutus is a stoic, coolly indifferent to portents and omens. Later in the play, though he has already learned that his wife is dead, he feigns ignorance so that he can demonstrate his absolute self-mastery: "Why farewell, Portia" (4.3.189). But the calculated demonstration already calls into question the authenticity of the principle, and the play repeatedly undermines anything that looks philosophically coherent.

None of the characters—certainly not Julius Caesar, Antony, or Cassius—embodies a stable position, let alone an abstract ideal. Brutus comes closest, and in the play's final moments Antony eulogizes him as "the noblest Roman of them all" (5.5.68). But these are the public pronouncements of the deeply cynical victor, and we have already seen from the inside how murky, confused, and conflicted are Brutus's thoughts. Nevertheless, in the midst of the uncertainty that besets every choice, it is necessary to decide what to do, and Brutus decides to kill Caesar. Believing that only this drastic step will save the republic, he lends his immense prestige to the group of conspirators, each of whom has his own tangled motives for action, and at the crucial moment, on the Ides of March, he joins the others in thrusting his knife into the body of his friend.

"Stoop, Romans, stoop," Brutus tells his fellow assassins, in the wake of their deed,

> And let us bathe our hands in Caesar's blood
> Up to the elbows and besmear our swords.
> Then walk we forth, even to the marketplace,
> And, waving our red weapons o'er our heads,

Let's all cry, "Peace, freedom, and liberty!"
(3.1.106–11)

Now and for generations to come, as he imagines it, they will be celebrated as the saviors of Rome. Their cause is just, and he is confident that it will be recognized as such precisely because they are not cynical politicians but men of noble ideals.

Except that it does not work out this way. The problem is not only that everyone's motives are inevitably more mixed than shouted slogans suggest, but also that real-world actions grounded on noble ideals may have unforeseen and ironic consequences. Brutus dreams that such ideals as honor, justice, and liberty can somehow exist in pure form, untouched by base calculations and messy compromises. Yet his staunchest attempt to act from pure principle is his refusal to kill Antony alongside Caesar, and that refusal is a political catastrophe. For Antony is not merely one of Caesar's loyal followers; he is a brilliant demagogue whose famous speech over Caesar's corpse—"Friends, Romans, countrymen, lend me your ears . . ." (3.2.71)—sparks the civil war that brings down the republic, the very institution the conspirators wished to save.

Shakespeare makes clear that Brutus's desire to keep his motives free from any taint of self-interest or violence is a mere fantasy. He longs to destroy the threat that Caesar represents—the threat of tyranny—without destroying Caesar, but even Brutus recognizes that this clean, bloodless defense of liberty is impossible:

> Oh, that we then could come by Caesar's spirit
> And not dismember Caesar! But, alas,
> Caesar must bleed for it. (2.1.169–71)

Shakespeare does not quite ridicule Brutus's refusal to permit the bloodletting that the other conspirators wish to undertake in the wake of the assassination. That refusal bespeaks a certain nobility of spirit that contrasts sharply with the cynical opportunism of Antony and his allies, who immediately seize the occasion to kill their enemies. But the dream of purity is hopelessly unrealistic and hedged about with irony. And it utterly fails to take into account the volatility of the mass of ordinary Romans.

Julius Caesar does not offer any solution to the psychological and political dilemmas it mercilessly probes. There is no moment of clear-eyed understanding, certainly not for Cassius (who commits suicide because he hopelessly misconstrues the outcome of the swirling battle at Philippi) or for Brutus, who is haunted by Caesar's ghost. What the tragedy offers instead is an unprecedented representation of political uncertainty, confusion, and blindness. The attempt to avert a possible constitutional crisis, were Caesar to decide to assume tyrannical powers, precipitates the collapse of the state. The very act that was meant to save the republic turns out to destroy it. Caesar is dead, but by the end of the play Caesarism is triumphant.

Ten

RESISTIBLE RISE

SOCIETIES, LIKE INDIVIDUALS, generally protect themselves from sociopaths. We would not have been able to survive as a species had we not developed the skill to identify and deal with noxious threats from within as well as without. Communities are usually alert to the danger posed by certain people in their midst and contrive to isolate or expel them. This is why tyranny is not the norm of social organization.

In special circumstances, however, protection proves more difficult than it would at first seem, for some of the dangerous qualities found in a potential tyrant may be useful. Shakespeare's great historical example of this double-edged utility is Caius Martius, better known as Coriolanus, whose fierce aggression, imperiousness, and indifference to pain made him an immensely successful warrior in defense of Rome in the fifth century B.C.E. The playwright found the outline of the story in one of his favorite sources, Plutarch's *Lives*, and he fashioned it into the last tragedy he ever wrote.

Coriolanus is set in the very distant past, but the play

obliquely addressed immediate and pressing concerns. Food shortages in England, linked to periodic bad harvests, had for generations led to noisy popular protests, with mobs crying out for emergency relief supplies. In 1607, a full-scale revolt erupted in the Midlands, spreading quickly from Northamptonshire to Leicestershire and Warwickshire. The angry crowds, thousands strong, denounced the hated practice of grain hoarding in the hope of a higher price and demanded that local landlords stop the illegal enclosure of common lands.

The principal rebel leader was John Reynolds, called "Captain Pouch" because he carried a small bag whose magical contents were supposed to defend the protesters from harm. Reynolds urged his followers to be nonviolent, and for the most part they contented themselves with tearing down the hedges and filling in the ditches with which the landlords were attempting to enclose, for their own profit, lands that had belonged to everyone. The local constables stayed calm, but property owners were deeply alarmed. Shakespeare himself had every reason to share their concern, since he owned lands in Warwickshire and in a modest way he had himself been hoarding grain. The question, therefore, was how to respond to the disorder.

The elites urgently debated the best strategy for dealing with the protests, with some advocating food handouts and the cessation of enclosures, others urging tough measures. Do not attempt "any persuasion at all," the Earl of Shrewsbury wrote to his brother the Earl of Kent, until "you have some

40 or 50 horse well-appointed, which will run over and cut in pieces a thousand of such naked rogues as these."[19] This grim argument was, in effect, the one that prevailed. In June 1607, dozens of protesters were killed by the landlords' armed servants, and Captain Pouch was seized and hanged. (According to a contemporary chronicler, his pouch contained "only a piece of green cheese.")The Midland Revolt came to an end.

SHAKESPEARE'S PLAY OPENS with a food riot in ancient Rome, and Coriolanus is very much of the Earl of Shrewsbury's opinion about the best way to handle the situation. If his fellow patricians would only set aside their misguided compassion, he declares,

> And let me use my sword, I'd make a quarry
> With thousands of these quartered slaves as high
> As I could pitch my lance. (*Coriolanus* 1.1.189–91)

To his intense disgust, the patricians decide instead to appease the mob by giving them a measure of political representation in the form of two tribunes to speak for their interests. In Coriolanus's view, two tribunes are two too many. The common people, he thinks, should have no representation at all; they should simply have their fates dictated to them.

The patrician party—the party of "the right-hand file," as one of its principal spokesmen calls it—has a single dominant interest: to ensure (through what we would now call fiscal policy) a grossly unequal distribution of resources and to protect the property its members have amassed. To this interest, the patricians are willing to sacrifice virtually everything else. They are certainly willing to sacrifice the well-being and even the lives of the poor.

The wealthy aristocrats depend on the labor of the lower classes—the agricultural labor of those who sweat in the fields outside the city walls; the labor of the workmen, artisans, and servants within the city; and the labor of the common soldiers who swell the ranks of the army that defends the city against its enemies. It is for this reason that, when the poor, in their desperation, finally put down their tools and riot, the patricians concede to at least a few of their demands. But even this concession is not an actual acknowledgment of dependence. On the contrary, the elite perceive the poor, and the urban poor in particular, as a mere drain upon the economy, a swarm of idle mouths demanding to be fed. After all, most of the land and what it produces, along with the houses, the factories, and almost everything else, belongs to the patricians. To them, looking down from the top of this mountain of possessions, the poor, who own virtually nothing, seem like parasites. So, too, the patrician soldiers: trained from childhood in the arts of war, well-armed, mounted on fierce war horses, shining in battle and honored with medals, they see the poor—who merely drag up the siege equipment, carry the gear, and try to shield themselves from the deadly rain of arrows—as a pack of cowards.

The closest any of the patricians come, in Shakespeare's

play, to acknowledging obligation to the poor is a highly emblematic moment in which Coriolanus, having captured the enemy city Corioles (from whose conquest he derives his honorific title), asks his commanding general for a favor. "Take't, 'tis yours," the grateful general says. "What is't?" Coriolanus replies that he had been billeted in Corioles at "a poor man's house; he used me kindly" (1.9.79–81). His host has now been taken prisoner by the Romans. Being led off to whatever fate the conquerors had in store for their captives, the man spotted his erstwhile guest and cried out to him, but at that moment of recognition, Coriolanus rushed off to do battle against the enemy captain: "wrath o'erwhelmed my pity." Now, he asks, "I request you/To give my poor host freedom" (1.9.84–85). The general is moved—"Were he the butcher of my son, he should/Be free as is the wind" (1.9.86–87)—and asks for the man's name. Unfortunately, Coriolanus has forgotten it.

For the patricians, the plebeians have no names. Still, the poor people who riot for bread in Rome at least manage to make their complaints heard. If only the patricians were willing to release it, they shout, there is more than enough grain stored up, despite the bad harvests, to prevent starvation. The wealthy, however, would rather let the grain rot in the granaries than undermine its market price. And, beyond the greed of hoarders, the fundamental problem is that the state's whole economic system has been designed in such a way as not to temper but to exacerbate the income gap between rich and poor.

Though they are responsible for this system, having drawn

up the tax code and the financial regulations, the patricians, of course, would never admit that such was their intention. In their genial spokesman, Menenius Agrippa, Shakespeare draws a deft portrait of a successful conservative politician, altogether in the camp of the rich but adept at presenting himself as the people's friend. Exuding his deep sympathy for their plight, he reminds the rioters—"my good friends, mine honest neighbors" (1.1.55), as he calls them—that the patricians can hardly be held responsible for the bad weather that has caused the famine. Violence will achieve nothing. He counsels patience and prayer, along with trust in the "charitable care" that the wealthy always take for those less fortunate than themselves.

"They ne'er cared for us yet," a heckler in the crowd shouts;

> Suffer us to famish, and their storehouses crammed
> with grain; make edicts for usury to support usurers;
> repeal daily any wholesome act established against
> the rich; and provide more piercing statutes daily to
> chain up and restrain the poor. (1.1.72–77)

The charges leveled here by the anonymous citizen are trenchant and coherent. We are not in the world of Jack Cade and his drunken mob baying for blood. Another voice in the crowd even offers a theory, bitter yet plausible, of why those who have more wealth than they need or could possibly use would complacently allow others to go hungry. "The lean-ness that afflicts us," he notes at the scene's opening, the visible fact "of our misery, is as an inventory to particularize their abundance" (1.1.17–18). The spectacle of so many poor make the rich feel even richer.

Menenius counters with a celebrated fable, an allegorical tale of a rebellion against the belly by other parts of the body. These body parts did all the hard work, such as seeing, hearing, and walking; the belly, they complained, did nothing but sit around and eat. Of course, as the fable goes on to suggest, the belly, far from being idle, is really "the storehouse and the shop/Of the whole body." It works constantly, though invisibly, to distribute essential nourishment to every part. The patrician senators of Rome, Menenius insists, are precisely this distribution point. They turn out to be the source of every good thing in the lives of the people:

> you shall find
> No public benefit which you receive
> But it proceeds or comes from them to you
> And no way from yourselves. (1.1.142–45)

In this account, it is entirely proper that everything flows first into the coffers of the wealthy; properly digested by them, it then trickles down in appropriate amounts to everyone else.

Whether the hungry rioters would have been persuaded by this fanciful apologia for elite consumption is left unclear. At this point Menenius's friend Coriolanus appears, and the conservative politician suddenly drops the pretense of folksy affection for the masses. The martial hero does not traffic in any such pretenses. Refusing to put on the kinder, gentler mask of the politically adept conservatives, he speaks out instead in the voice of an alternative right-hand file that, far from dressing its policies in genial fables, is itching to unleash a massacre.

He might have carried out his threat had not news arrived of an impending attack on Rome by its chief enemy, the Volsces. The news makes him happy, not merely because war is his vocation but also because it will, with any luck, sweep away the lives of a significant number of the "rabble." "I am glad on't," he exults, for now "we shall ha' means to vent/ Our musty superfluity" (1.1.216–17). For this fierce warrior, the poor—those who are now on the dole—are like scraps of food that have turned moldy. The best thing is to get rid of them and open the windows.

The merciless psychology and politics of the fatherless Coriolanus all seem to derive from his mother, the formidable Volumnia. "When yet he was but tender-bodied and the only son of my womb, when youth with comeliness plucked all gaze his way, when—for a day of kings' entreaties—a mother should not sell him an hour from her beholding," she boasts, "I . . . was pleased to let him seek danger where he was like to find fame." She raised her son to focus, as she does, on a supreme goal: military glory. "To a cruel war, I sent him" (1.3.5–12).

Volumnia's passionate concern for her child's renown and

fame has something ghoulish about it. The only son of her
womb, as she puts it, is an object, a mirror in which she sees
her own importance; nothing else about him matters. She has
no maternal interest in protecting her son's "tender" body.
On the contrary, she glories in the scars he bears from his
encounters with Rome's enemies. To her, war wounds are
beautiful:

> The breasts of Hecuba
> When she did suckle Hector looked not lovelier
> Than Hector's forehead when it spit forth blood
> At Grecian sword contemning. (1.3.37–40)

Everything about the perversity of her son's upbringing is
concentrated in her strange transformation of the image of
a mother breast-feeding a baby into the spectacle of blood
spurting from a gash.

In a macabre scene, Volumnia and Menenius, who is a
kind of adoptive father to Coriolanus, excitedly share the
news of his latest accomplishments—which is to say, his latest wounds. "Where is he wounded?" Menenius eagerly
asks. "I'th'shoulder and i'th'left arm" (2.1.132–36), Volumnia
replies. She is already thinking ahead to the political advantage the injuries will confer upon her son when he offers
himself as a candidate for consul, republican Rome's highest
office: "There will be large cicatrices to show the people when
he shall stand for his place." The two old people continue their
grotesque inventory:

VOLUMNIA: He had, before this last expedition,
   twenty-five wounds upon him.
MENENIUS: Now it's twenty-seven. Every gash
   was an enemy's grave. (2.1.136–45)

It hardly seems like they are describing a human body. When
the noise of trumpets signal Coriolanus's approach, his mother
describes her son in terms more suitable for a weapon:

> Before him
> He carries noise, and behind him he leaves tears.
> Death, that dark spirit, in 's nervy [i.e., muscular]
>   arm doth lie,
> Which, being advanced, declines, and then men
>   die. (2.1.147–50)

Ever the dutiful son, Coriolanus has not only acquired
the scars that so gratify his mother but also turned himself
into the inhuman object she wishes him to be. In battle, as
his awestruck general describes him, "from face to foot/He
was a thing of blood" (2.2.105–6). And as he has been made
a "thing," so he makes others. For him the common people
are "slaves," "rabble," "curs," "scabs." He slashes, burns, and
kills everything in his path.

Near the beginning of the play, we see Coriolanus's
wife, Virgilia, conversing with a friend, who asks her how
her young son is doing. "Well, good madam," she politely
answers, but this reply does not suit the child's martial grand-

mother, Volumnia. "He had rather see the swords and hear a drum," she says proudly of her grandchild, "than look upon his schoolmaster" (1.3.52–53). This tiny glimpse back into the values of Coriolanus's own childhood is immediately reinforced by the friend, who goes on to relate an anecdote that she knows will please the grandmother. "I looked upon him o' Wednesday half an hour together" (1.3.55–56). What a "confirmed countenance"—a determined expression—the promising little grandson had! "I saw him run after a gilded butterfly, and when he caught it, he let it go again, and after it again, and over and over he comes, and up again, catched it again. Or whether his fall enraged him, or how 'twas, he did so set his teeth and tear it. Oh, I warrant, how he mammocked it!" (1.3.57–61).

Why does the child's mammocking a butterfly—tearing it to shreds—make it into the play? One of his "father's moods" (1.3.62), Volumnia delightedly responds. We cannot help but see Coriolanus as the product of a mother like Volumnia, just as we see him, even at his most terrifying, as an extremely dangerous version of a little boy. To be sure, he is a great warrior. People obey his orders and tremble before him. He wields the power of life and death. He can save cities or break them. He can exterminate families, threaten whole realms, cast a shadow over the entire known world. But the menace does not eradicate the perception of his childishness.

In civilized states, we expect leaders to have achieved at least a minimal level of adult self-control, and we hope as well for thoughtfulness, decency, respect for others, regard for institutions. Not so Coriolanus: here we are dealing instead with an overgrown child's narcissism, insecurity, cruelty, and folly, all unchecked by any adult's supervision and restraint. The adult who should have helped the child achieve maturity has either been completely missing or, if present at all, has reinforced the child's worst qualities.

The suite of traits brought forth by his upbringing—a proneness to rage, a merciless penchant for bullying, an absence of empathy, a refusal to compromise, a compulsive desire to wield power over others—helps to explain Coriolanus's success in war. But the question on which the plot turns is what happens when such a personality seeks to wield supreme authority not on the battlefield, at the head of the Roman army, but in the state.

After acquitting himself brilliantly in battle, Coriolanus comes home to immense and well-deserved popular acclaim. "I have seen/The dumb men throng to see him," a messenger reports,

> and the blind
> To hear him speak. Matrons flung gloves,
> Ladies and maids their scarves and handkerchiefs
> Upon him as he passed. The nobles bended
> As to Jove's statue, and the commons made
> A shower and thunder with their caps and shouts.
>   (2.1.249–55)

He is the city's savior.

This is the perfect moment, as his mother and other leaders of the patrician party grasp, for Coriolanus to stand for election as consul. To be sure, his political views are quite extreme, and he voices them without restraint, but the wealthy now regret the concessions they made under the pressure of the urban riots. As consul, Coriolanus would be in a position to take back what has been given away. From the beginning, he has voiced steadfast opposition to giving the plebeians any political representation and to creating any safety net at all. "They said they were an-hungry," he remarks contemptuously, describing the starving crowds,

> sighed forth proverbs
> That hunger broke stone walls, that dogs must eat,
> That meat was made for mouths, that the gods
>   sent not
> Corn for the rich men only. (1.1.196–99)

For him, these are the voices of the "musty superfluity"; Rome would be better if they were allowed to starve to death.

In the wake of the Volscian wars, even Menenius, who took care to cloak his right-hand-file views with a genial air of populism, has adopted a harder edge. There is no longer any reason to compromise with or appease the lower classes. "You wear out a good wholesome forenoon in hearing a cause between an orange-wife and a faucet-seller," he says, mocking the tribunes. "More of your conversation would infect my brain," he sneers, as he parts from them, "being the herdsmen of the beastly plebeians" (2.1.62–63, 85–86). There is a new tone in Roman political life, one that is meaner and that flirts with violence.

Volumnia thinks that now, when the political opportunity has arisen, her son will adapt to circumstances, enter politics, and solicit the votes of the common people. But he initially refuses to do what his mother asks. After all, it was she, as Coriolanus points out, who taught him to call those very people "woolen vassals, things created/To buy and sell with groats" (3.2.9–10)— that is, for pennies. It was she who made him, from earliest childhood, into the inflexible, angry, proud destroyer that he is. In resisting the call to compromise, he is being true to himself, which is to say true to his upbringing. It is only under her relentless pressure that he agrees very reluctantly to stand for office.

There are other candidates for consul, but the war hero Coriolanus is the overwhelming favorite. His candidacy sails through the Senate; all that remains is for him to obtain the majority vote of the common people, and, given his spectacular combat record and his utter indifference to the spoils of war, that seems virtually assured. He has only to go through the formality of presenting himself to the people and showing them his battle scars. Of course, in principle the voters could still reject him; they know perfectly well that he is not their friend. Still, genuinely grateful for his military service to Rome, many are prepared to give him their votes—their "voices"—against their own class interests.

The wealthy patricians in this play regard the poor as

worthless, but the reverse is not true. Shakespeare conjures up the conversations going on throughout the city, as humble people attempt to balance self-interest and obligation, rights and indebtedness. "If he do require our voices," one of the plebeians says, "we ought not to deny him." "We may, sir," another counters, "if we will." "We have the power in ourselves to do it," replies a third, "but it is a power that we have no power to do" (2.3.1–5). These are, as Shakespeare depicts them, the small but precious perplexities of free elections.

The whole procedure depends on all parties sharing a fundamental respect for the system. Quite simply, Coriolanus needs, in the customary, time-honored way, to ask for the people's votes. His anti-democratic extremism, however, cannot abide even this minimal show of respect. To the wealthy senators, men of his class and his values, he acknowledges an obligation: "I do owe them still/My life and services" (2.2.130–31). To the common people he refuses to recognize any bond at all.

Here is where the people's tribunes, the hard-bitten professional politicians Sicinius and Brutus, prove their mettle. Shakespeare is not in the least sentimental about their motives or methods. Cynical, conniving, and manipulative, they are career politicians, bent principally on protecting their own positions. The people they represent are easily swayed. At one moment cheering the war hero Coriolanus, at the next they are shouting, "Down with him!" and calling for his execution or exile. They seem hopelessly confused. Nonetheless, what the tribunes make the people see is the plain truth: the patrician party, of which Coriolanus is the champion, is in fact their enemy.

Calculating correctly that Coriolanus will be brought down by his arrogance, his extremism, and his violent temper, they steadfastly insist that proper procedures be observed: the candidate will not be exempted from the obligation to solicit the popular vote. Intensely eager to have their champion elected to the consulship, the patricians plead with Coriolanus to moderate his pride and go through the charade of addressing the people. "You must desire them/To think upon you," Menenius tells him. "Think upon me?" Coriolanus fumes; "Hang 'em!" "Pray you, speak to 'em, I pray you," the frustrated Menenius urges, "In wholesome manner." "Bid them wash their faces/And keep their teeth clean" is his sneering reply (2.3.51–58).

Nothing tempers Coriolanus's obnoxiousness, and yet the play is oddly sympathetic to him, at least compared with the others of his class. The patricians urge him to set aside his most deeply held convictions for the purpose of getting elected. They want him to lie and to pander and to play the demagogue. Once he is securely in office, there will be plenty of time for him to resume his actual stance and to roll back the concessions that have been made to the poor. It is the most familiar of political games: the plutocrat, born into every privilege and inwardly contemptuous of those beneath him, who mouths the rhetoric of populism during the electoral campaign, abandoning it as soon as it has served his purposes. The Romans had boiled it all down to a conventional performance, comparable to a well-coiffed politician's donning of a hard hat at a rally held at a construction site: the candidate for office would set aside his richly dyed robes and, entering the marketplace, put on a threadbare white garment, "the napless vesture of humility" (2.1.222). Then, if he had any battle scars, he would show them, like a résumé, and solicit the people's votes.

Coriolanus finds the whole charade disgusting. He makes an effort to do what his party pleads with him to do, but his gorge rises at it. He tries, as he puts it, to "counterfeit the bewitchment of some popular man"—that is, to imitate the charismatic style of a successful politician. His attempt to "practice the insinuating nod" (2.3.93–95), however, is so fake, so manifestly against his whole being, that it fails. At first the people are inclined to give him the benefit of the doubt and to promise him their votes, but they come away from the marketplace rally with the queasy sense that they have been mocked. It is easy enough for Brutus and Sicinius, reminding the crowd that Coriolanus "ever spake against/Your liberties" (2.3.171–72), to turn their queasiness into second thoughts, regret, and a withdrawal of support.

The whole sequence is a lesson in bare-knuckles politics, as Shakespeare understood it. What seems settled can quickly come apart. It looks, for a moment, as if the patrician senators have won: as they had advised him to do, Coriolanus has stood in the marketplace and successfully solicited the requisite number of "voices." But there is one last step: a largely pro forma official confirmation of the vote. With their backs to the wall, Brutus and Sicinius use this procedural formality to force the whole process to grind to a halt.

The tribunes are as calculating and deceptive as the elite against whom they are fighting. Tyranny cannot be stopped, Shakespeare must have thought, if the democratic opposition is so high-minded that it is powerless to counter the political conniving that leads up to a seizure of power. Coriolanus's wealthy allies urge him to cloak his actual views in order to be elected. The tribunes urge the people to cloak the role that they, the tribunes, have played in eliciting and organizing the last-minute shift. "Lay the fault on us" (2.3.225), they slyly suggest: the voters should claim that their leaders pressured them into supporting Coriolanus but that now, reflecting on his inveterate enmity and his mockery, the people have revoked that support.

When the voters follow these instructions, Coriolanus is enraged and gives full voice to the hatred of democracy that the elite desperately wished him to hide until the election was over. Attempts to sooth the multitude, he fumes, only encourage "rebellion, insolence, sedition" (3.1.68). The poor are "measles"; letting them get anywhere close to power is inviting infection. His friends try to shut him up. Though these are views they may share among themselves, they do not wish to make them public. But Coriolanus will not stop. There cannot, he declares, be two authorities in the state. Either the patricians rule over the plebeians, as they should, or the whole social order will be turned upside down: "You are plebeians/If they be senators" (3.1.98–99). As for the social

safety net—the distribution of free food in order to prevent starvation—it has only "nourished disobedience, fed/
The ruin of the state" (3.1.114–15). After hearing this rant,
the tribune Brutus asks, reasonably enough, "Why shall the
people give/One that speaks thus their voice?" (3.1.115–16).

For once, thanks to Coriolanus's complete lack of restraint,
everything is out in the open. The more moderate senators
had been willing to concede just barely enough to ward off
a major public health emergency and massive social protest.
Although they contrived to constrain the popular vote, they
allowed at least a semblance of representation. But for Coriolanus, who cannot abide the hypocrisy and temporizing of
his own class, that "just barely enough" is far too much. His
modest proposal: let the poor starve. Famine will reduce the
number of drones, and those who survive will be less inclined
to ask for handouts. Those handouts, he thinks, only make
the lower classes less self-reliant; the entire welfare system is
a kind of drug.

What is needed, he openly declares, is for the patricians to
have courage enough to take away what the plebeians think
they want but what is actually, he believes, hurting them
and hurting the state. This means eliminating not only the
free food but also the whole institution of tribunes who give
the poor a political voice. It is not enough to restrict popular
representation—in effect, to practice the Roman equivalent
of voter suppression, intimidation, redistricting, and the like.
Coriolanus proposes something far more radical. "Pluck out/
The multitudinous tongue," he urges, "let them not lick/

The sweet which is their poison" (3.1.152–54). Essentially, he wants to tear up the Roman constitution.

The tribunes immediately charge Coriolanus with treason. They demand that he be arrested "as a traitorous innovator,/A foe to th' public weal" (3.1.171–72). And the truth is that his radical proposals threaten the elite—whose carefully constructed ideological cover they tear open—as much as the plebeians. "On both sides more respect," begs Menenius, when the two opposed parties come to blows. The conflict, one of the senators says, threatens "to unbuild the city and to lay all flat." Sicinius counters, "What is the city but the people?," and his followers take up the phrase like a slogan: "The people are the city," "The people are the city" (3.1.177–94).

Civil war now looms, and regardless of the military might of Coriolanus and the patricians, sheer numbers favor the enraged populace. "'Tis odds beyond arithmetic," the patrician general Cominius soberly observes. "Could he not speak 'em fair," asks the frustrated Menenius, to whom it falls once again to try to appease the mob (3.1.238, 56). This time he undertakes to bring Coriolanus back to the marketplace, to submit himself to the law and answer the charges against him.

Persuading him to do so is no easy task. In this attempt, Menenius is joined by Volumnia, who shares his frustration that the stiff-necked Coriolanus could not dissemble just long enough to be elected. "Lesser had been/The taxings of your dispositions," she tells her son, "if/You had not showed them how ye were disposed/Ere they lacked power to cross you" (3.2.20–23). Coriolanus's response is "Let them hang," to which his mother adds, "Ay, and burn too" (3.2.23–24). But cursing the people will not solve the problem. The only intelligent course of action, she says, is for Coriolanus to do what, in effect, the elite have always known how to do:

> to speak
> To th' people, not by your own instruction,
> Nor by th' matter which your heart prompts you,
> But with such words that are but roted in
> Your tongue, though but bastards and syllables
> Of no allowance to your bosom's truth.
>
> (3.2.52–57)

Just lie. Everyone shares this view, she assures him: "Your wife, your son, these senators, the nobles" (3.2.65).

It is in Coriolanus's power to solve the crisis he has provoked. The price he needs to pay is simply to behave, for once, like a politician. But for him this price is unbearably high. Everything in Coriolanus's being—the fierce integrity and pride and spirit of command he has imbibed from his mother—rebels against playing so degrading a part. And the conflict is all the more unbearable because it is precisely his mother who now urges him to debase himself. "I prithee now, sweet son," she tells him,

as thou hast said
My praises made thee first a soldier, so
To have my praise for this, perform a part
Thou hast not done before. (3.2.107–10)

Volumnia understands perfectly well that her son's sense of his manhood is at stake and that he has shaped his whole identity from the beginning by trying to please her. The scars that cover his body were never meant for theatrical display before the people; they were adornments offered only to her. But now, devastatingly enough, she tells him that he has been trying too hard: "You might have been enough the man you are/With striving less to be so" (3.2.19–20). Or, rather, he hears from his mother a demand for a different, even more painful form of masochism. She wants him, in his view, to be a beggar, a knave, a weeping schoolboy, or a whore. Worse still, she wants his "throat of war" to be turned "into a pipe/Small as an eunuch" (3.2.112–14). All right, he says, for her and her alone, he will in effect castrate himself: "Mother, I am going to the marketplace" (3.2.131).

In the event, as with his earlier effort to solicit votes, Coriolanus's attempt to play the politician is a disaster. The tribunes know that he is psychologically unstable, and they exploit his weakness perfectly. They denounce his attack on the time-honored structures of government as an attempt to set himself up as a tyrant: "you have contrived to take/From Rome all seasoned office and to wind/Yourself into a power tyrannical" (3.3.61–63). Therefore, they declare, you are "a traitor to the people." The charge of treason is enough to send him back into an uncontrollable rage, and the result is a sentence of banishment from the city.

Having brought about what they set out to accomplish, the wily tribunes beat a strategic retreat: "Now we have shown our power," one of them says. "Let us seem humbler after it is done/Than when it was a-doing" (4.2.3–5). But though the play always shows them to be crafty, it does not prove them to be far from the truth. Coriolanus had indeed urged the patricians to disenfranchise the lower classes. If he had been elected consul, he would certainly have attempted to do just that. And even in the wake of his banishment, the threat is not over. A Roman spy, meeting his Volscian contact, reports that the nobles "are in a ripe aptness to take all power from the people and to pluck from them their tribunes forever" (4.3.19–21).

What is baffling about this upper-class plotting is that Rome, after Coriolanus's banishment, has never seemed more prosperous for everyone. Instead of protests and rioting, the common people are a model of tranquil contentment. One of the tribunes remarks cannily that this peace and quietness makes Coriolanus's patrician friends

> Blush that the world goes well, who rather had,
> Though they themselves did suffer by't, behold
> Dissentious numbers pest'ring streets than see
> Our tradesmen singing in their shops and going
> About their functions friendly. (4.6.5–9)

It is a perverse but familiar pattern: the party of privilege argues that it needs authoritarian power so that it can preserve order in the state. Coriolanus speaks for his class when he tells the people that only "the noble Senate . . . /Under the gods, keep you in awe, which else/Would feed on one another" (1.1.177–79). Then when the wealthy are proven wrong—when the state, rich and poor alike, turns out to thrive under a more democratic system—they long for the disorder they promised to quell.

And what of Coriolanus? His rage was prompted by the charge that he was a traitor to the commonwealth—as if he, who had shed so much of his noble blood for Rome, were no better than the lower-class spy we see reporting to the Volscians. Yet in the wake of his banishment, it is precisely to the Volscians that Coriolanus turns. "My birthplace hate I," he says, "and my love's upon/This enemy town" (4.4.23–24).

The plot twist is worth dwelling upon. It is as if the leader of a political party long identified with hatred of Russia— forever saber-rattling and accusing the rival politicians of treason—should secretly make his way to Moscow and offer his services to the Kremlin. Whatever had been the source of Coriolanus's martial heroism, it was certainly not love for the people and not even loyalty to the abstract idea of Rome. He had once felt a bond to his fellow patricians, but in his view his social class has forsaken him, allowing him "by th' voice of slaves to be/Whooped out of Rome" (4.5.76–77). His bitter words provide a clear view into his vision of his homeland: the common people, whose votes he was supposed to solicit, are all "slaves"; the "dastard nobles" are cowards who refused at the crucial moment to make the streets flow with blood to prevent his humiliating banishment. Now he longs for revenge against his entire "cankered country" (4.5.74, 90).

When Coriolanus arrives in Antium, the Volscians' capital, the enemy general Tullius Aufidius could rightly kill him, for the Roman warrior has shed much of their blood. But Aufidius grasps that he can make good use of the banished man's rage against his erstwhile countrymen. "Most absolute sir," Aufidius calls him, giving him command of half of the Volscian army and licensing him to devise the military campaign, "As best thou are experienced, since thou know'st/Thy country's strength and weakness" (4.5.138–39).

At first, when rumors of Coriolanus's betrayal and an impending attack under his leadership begin to circulate in Rome, the tribunes refuse to believe them. With the city prosperous and at peace, they think that such fears are fake news, invented by certain patrician factions "only that the weaker sort may wish" (4.6.70) Coriolanus home again. Even Menenius believes the rumors to be unlikely, since there is no way that the bitter enemies, Coriolanus and Aufidius, can form an alliance. But when it becomes clear that the approaching enemy army is not fake news, the patrician response is instructive. They do not cry out against Coriolanus's treachery and curse him for his violent betrayal of everything he had professed to love and defend. They turn instead on the plebeians: "You have made good work,/You and your apron-men," Menenius jeers at the tribunes. "You that stood so much/

Upon the voice of occupation and/The breath of garlic-eaters"
(4.6.95–98). It is all the fault of working people, with their
stinking breaths and their presumptuous insistence on being
heard. They—and not Coriolanus—have betrayed Rome.

The tribunes try to reassure their constituents. "Be not
dismayed," they tell them; the terrifying reports come from
a faction "that would be glad to have/This true which they
so seem to fear" (4.6.149–51). The observation is just—the
patricians so hate the plebeians that they perversely welcome
Coriolanus's treason—but the people are right to be afraid.
The play wryly sketches the immediate commencement of
historical revisionism. "I ever said we were i'th'wrong when
we banished him" (4.6.154–55), one of plebeians remarks. "So
did we all," adds another.

The climactic fifth act of Shakespeare's play confirms the
lack in Coriolanus of any loyalty to Rome, to the patrician
party, even to his friend Cominius or his surrogate father,
Menenius, or his wife, Virgilia. "Forgive my tyranny," he tells
his wife, "but do not say/For that, 'Forgive our Romans'"
(5.3.43–44). He is dead set against compromise. At the head
of the Volscian army, he is encamped at Rome's gates like
an implacable god of destruction, poised to burn the city to
the ground, cut the throats of the men, and haul the women
and children off to slavery. That he does not do so depends
entirely on the intercession of his mother. Volumnia shocks
him by kneeling down to him, at once begging and berating
him. It is, she says, as if a Volscian and not she had given birth
to Coriolanus: "This fellow had a Volscian to his mother"

(5.3.178). Against this appeal he is unable to remain firm: "O mother, mother!/What have you done?" (5.3.182–83). He spares the city and opts instead for a peace treaty.

Rome is saved, but for Coriolanus there is no triumphant return to his homeland. He had, after all, been on the brink of annihilating it. He opts instead to go back to Volscian Antium, though he knows that his situation is a precarious one. "You have won a happy victory to Rome," he tells his mother. "But for your son—believe it, oh, believe it—/Most dangerously you have with him prevailed" (5.3.186–88).

Aufidius, who has no desire to share power and credit with his erstwhile enemy, begins at once to plot Coriolanus's destruction. He needs to act quickly because the Roman general is popular with the Volscian people, to whom he has delivered, as he puts it, peace with honor. Before he can deliver the signed peace treaty to the Volscian Senate, Aufidius interrupts him:

> Read it not, noble lords,
> But tell the traitor in the highest degree
> He hath abused your powers. (5.6.83–85)

As with the Romans, so with the Volscians: Coriolanus hears himself accused of treason. Once again the word makes him explode in rage, but this time there will be no negotiation by his patrician friends and no mitigating sentence of banishment. Aufidius reminds the Volscians of where their true civic loyalty lies. Or, rather, he reminds them of their losses. "Tear him the pieces!" the crowd shouts, as each of them recalls someone whom Coriolanus has destroyed: "He killed my son!—My daughter!—He killed my cousin Marcus!—He killed my father!" The last words Coriolanus hears, as the conspirators close in upon him with their swords, sum up his cruel legacy: "Kill, kill, kill, kill, kill him!" (5.6.120–29).

At the play's climax, what saves Rome from Coriolanus's destructive power is the tyrant's own personality: the psychological damage that has made him what he is finally undoes him. "There's no man in the world," Volumnia says, "More bound to's mother" (5.3.158–59). The grateful senators urge the people to celebrate Coriolanus's mother as the city's heroic savior. But, well before the final scene at the gates, the city had been protected from tyranny first and foremost by its tribunes, the career politicians who roused the people into action. Ignoble and self-serving, these functionaries, akin to the much-maligned professional politicians of democratic congresses and parliaments everywhere, nonetheless stood up to the bullying warrior-chief and insisted on the rights of ordinary people—artisans and grocers, workmen and porters—to reconsider their votes. Without their stubborn insistence and their crafty maneuvering, Rome would have fallen into the hands of a man who affected "one sole throne/Without assistance" (4.6.33–34). Though no statue is erected in their honor, it is they who are the city's real saviors.

CODA

IT WAS ALL a long time ago, in a society with a very different political system, one that lacked the constitutional protection of free speech and the basic norms of democratic society. When Shakespeare was a child, a wealthy Catholic, John Felton, was drawn and quartered for posting a copy of a papal bull and for asserting "that the queen had never been true queen of England." A few years later, a Puritan, John Stubbs, had his right hand chopped off by the public executioner for writing a pamphlet that denounced the queen's proposed marriage to a French Catholic. The pamphlet's distributor was similarly maimed. Comparably severe punishments for acts of speech and writing that were adjudged criminal by the authorities continued all through the reigns of Elizabeth and James.

Shakespeare no doubt attended some of the ghastly spectacles. Along with marking the boundaries of acceptable expression that it behooved him to observe, they revealed a great deal about the human character at moments of insupportable pain and suffering. They revealed, as well, much about the fears and desires of the crowd, precisely the passions that were the playwright's stock-in-trade. His power as an artist derived from the people. He set himself the goal not to be a coterie writer, finding a niche in the household of a sophisticated patron, but a popular entertainer, luring the masses to part with their pennies in exchange for deep thrills.[20]

Those thrills frequently bordered on transgression—hence the constant calls by moralists, ministers, and civic officials to close all the theaters down. But Shakespeare understood where the danger lay. He certainly knew that it was treason "by writing, printing, preaching, speech, express words or sayings" to affirm that the sovereign is a "heretic, schismatic, tyrant, infidel, or usurper of the crown." And he knew that for a playwright, any critical reflections on powerful contemporary figures or on contested issues were at once alluring and risky. His colleague Thomas Nashe fled from an arrest warrant for sedition; Ben Jonson languished in prison on similar charges; Thomas Kyd died shortly after being tortured in the course of an investigation into his roommate, Christopher Marlowe; Marlowe was stabbed to death by an agent in the queen's secret service. It was important to tread carefully.

Master of the oblique angle, Shakespeare prudently projected his imagination away from his immediate circumstances. And avoiding imprisonment was not his only motive. He was not an embittered malcontent, set on undermining the authority of this lord and that bishop, let alone challenging his sovereign or stirring up sedition. He was on the way to making himself a wealthy man, with steady income from playhouse receipts, real estate investments, commodity trading, and occasional quiet money-lending. Disorder was not in his interest. His works bespeak a deep aversion to violence—even, or perhaps especially, so-called principled violence—directed against established leaders.

But his works bespeak, as well, an aversion to the government-sanctioned platitudes rehearsed in texts like the "Homilies on Obedience," reactionary commonplaces par-roted by orators at public events like elections and execu-tions, and expatiated on by time-serving priests eager to snatch a superior benefice. Perhaps Shakespeare thought that the official strategy—the celebration of those in authority, a belligerent refusal to acknowledge gross economic ineq-uity, the perpetual invocation of God's partisan support for whoever was on top, and the demonizing of even the most modest skepticism—had the very opposite effect of what was intended. For it only reinforced a sense that the whole system of values—who is honorable and who is base, what counts as goodness and what is branded as evil, where the boundaries are drawn between truth and lies—was a monstrous fraud. It was Sir Thomas More, from whom Shakespeare borrowed so much of his portrait of Richard III, who put the matter most clearly almost a hundred years earlier: "When I consider any social system that prevails in the modern world," More wrote in *Utopia*, "I can't, so help me God, see it as anything but a conspiracy of the rich."

Shakespeare found a way to say what he needed to say. He managed to have someone stand up onstage and tell the two thousand listeners—some of whom were government agents—that "a dog's obeyed in office." The rich get away with what is brutally punished in the poor. "Plate sins with gold," his character continued,

> And the strong lance of justice hurtless breaks:
> Arm it in rags, a pigmy's straw does pierce it.

If you said words like these at the tavern, you stood a good chance of having your ears cut off. But day after day they were spoken in public, and the police were never called. Why not? Because the person who spoke them was Lear in his madness (*King Lear* 4.5.153, 160–61).

As we have seen, Shakespeare reflected throughout his life on the ways communities disintegrate. Endowed with an uncannily acute perception of human character and with rhetorical skills that would be the envy of any demagogue, he deftly sketched the kind of person who surges up in troubled times to appeal to the basest instincts and to draw upon the deepest anxiety of his contemporaries. A society locked into bitterly factionalized party politics, in his view, is particularly vulnerable to the fraudulent populism. And there are always instigators who arouse tyrannical ambition, and enablers, people who perceive the danger posed by this ambition but who think that they will be able to control the successful tyrant and to profit from his assault on established institutions.

The playwright repeatedly depicted the chaos that ensues

when tyrants, who generally have no administrative competence and no vision for constructive change, actually get possession of power. Even relatively healthy and stable societies, he thought, have few resources that enable them to ward off damage from someone sufficiently ruthless and unscrupulous; nor are they well-equipped to deal effectively with legitimate rulers who begin to show signs of unstable and irrational behavior.

Shakespeare never looked away from the horrible consequences visited upon societies that fall into the hands of tyrants. "Alas, poor country," laments one of the characters in Macbeth's Scotland,

> Almost afraid to know itself. It cannot
> Be called our mother, but our grave, where
> nothing
> But who knows nothing is once seen to smile;
> Where sighs and groans and shrieks that rend the air
> Are made, not marked; where violent sorrow seems
> A modern ecstasy. (*Macbeth* 4.3.165–70)

Shakespeare registered, as well, the full measure of the violence and misery that are generally required to get rid of those who cause such suffering. But he was not without hope. He thought that the way forward was not assassination, a desperate measure that in his view usually brought about the very thing it was most attempting to prevent. Rather, as he imagined toward the end of his career, the best hope lay in the sheer unpredictability of collective life, its refusal to march in lockstep to any one person's orders. The incalculable number of factors constantly in play make it impossible for an idealist or a tyrant, a Brutus or a Macbeth, to remain securely in charge of the course of events or to see, as Lady Macbeth dreams she does, "The future in the instant" (1.5.56).

As a playwright, Shakespeare strikingly embraced this unpredictability. He wrote plays that intertwined multiple plots, jumbled together kings and clowns, routinely violated generic expectations, and conspicuously ceded the control of interpretation to actors and audiences. There is in this theatrical practice an underlying trust that an extremely diverse, random body of spectators will ultimately work things out. Shakespeare's contemporary Ben Jonson once floated the fantasy that the members of the audience should be permitted to assess a play according to how much they paid for their seats: "It shall be lawful for any man to judge his six pen'orth [i.e., pennyworth], his twelve pen'orth, so to his eighteen pence, two shillings, half a crown, to the value of his place."[21] Nothing could be further from Shakespeare's evident conviction that everyone in the theater has an equal right to form an opinion and that the results in the aggregate, however messy, will finally confirm the success or failure of the enterprise.

A comparable conviction seems to underlie the depiction in *Coriolanus* of the city's narrow escape from tyranny, an escape that emerges from a confused tangle of causes: the autocratic hero's psychological instability, his mother's persuasive power, the small measure of agency conferred upon

the people, the behavior of the voters and their elected leaders. The playwright knew that it is easy to become cynical
about these leaders and to despair about the all-too-human
men and women who place their trust in them. The leaders
are often compromised and corruptible; the crowd is often
foolish, ungrateful, easily misled by demagogues, and slow
to understand where its real interests lie. There are periods, sometimes extended periods, during which the cruelest motives of the basest people seem to be triumphant.
But Shakespeare believed that the tyrants and their minions
would ultimately fail, brought down by their own viciousness
and by a popular spirit of humanity that could be suppressed
but never completely extinguished. The best chance for the
recovery of collective decency lay, he thought, in the political
action of ordinary citizens. He never lost sight of the people
who steadfastly remained silent when they were exhorted to
shout their support for the tyrant, or the servant who tried
to stop his vicious master from torturing a prisoner, or the
hungry citizen who demanded economic justice. "What is
the city but the people?"

ACKNOWLEDGMENTS

Not so very long ago, though it feels like a century has passed, I sat in a verdant garden in Sardinia and expressed my growing apprehensions about the possible outcome of an upcoming election. My historian friend Bernhard Jussen asked me what I was doing about it. "What can I do?" I asked. "You can write something," he said. And so I did.

That was the germ of the current book. And then, after the election confirmed my worst fears, my wife Ramie Targoff and son Harry, listening at the dinner table to my musings about Shakespeare's uncanny relevance to the political world in which we now find ourselves, urged me to pursue the subject. And so I have.

I extend my warmest thanks to Misha Teramura, a gifted literary historian, for his assistance in helping me understand the tangled relation between Shakespeare's *Richard II* and the fateful Essex rising and, more generally, for his sharp and always helpful responses to my chapters. I am grateful, too, to Jeffrey Knapp for a reading, at once generous and wisely critical, of the entire manuscript. Nicholas Utzig and Bailey Sincox greatly helped me with research in Tudor treason law and the theatrical representation of tyranny. My friends and frequent teaching partners Luke Menand and Joseph Koerner have been an inexhaustible source of inspiration to me, in the classroom and out. As always, there is a much wider circle of indebtedness to acknowledge, including, notably, Howard Jacobson, Meg Koerner, Thomas Laqueur, Sigrid Rausing, Michael Sexton, James Shapiro, and Michael Witmore. I have a bond of friendship and indebtedness to a large circle of Shakespeareans across the world, including (though not at all limited to) F. Murray Abraham, Hélio Alves, John Andrews, Oliver Arnold, Jonathan Bate, Shaul Bassi, Simon Russell Beale, Catherine Belsey, David Bergeron, David Bevington, Maryam Beyad, Mark Burnett, William Carroll, Roger Chartier, Walter Cohen, Rosy Colombo, Bradin Cormack, Jonathan Crewe, Brian Cummings, Trudy Darby, Anthony Dawson, Margreta de Grazia, Maria del Sapio, Jonathan Dollimore, John Drakakis, Katherine Eggert, Lars Engle, Lukas Erne, Ewan Fernie, Mary Floyd-Wilson, Indira Ghose, José González, Suzanne Gossett, Hugh Grady, Richard Halpern, Jonathan Gill Harris, Elizabeth Hanson, Atsuhiro Hirota, Rhema Hokama, Peter Holland, Jean Howard, Peter Hulme, Glen Hutchins, Grace Ioppolo, Farah Karim-Cooper, David Kastan, Takayuki Katsuyama, Philippa Kelly, Yu Jin Ko, Paul Kottman, Tony Kushner, François Laroque, George Logan, Julia Lupton, Laurie Maguire, Lawrence Manley, Leah Marcus, Katharine Maus, Richard McCoy, Gordon McMullan, Stephen Mullaney, Karen Newman, Zorica Nikolic, Stephen Orgel, Gail Paster, Lois Potter, Peter Platt, Richard Wilson, Mary Beth Rose, Mark Rylance, Elizabeth Samet, David Schalkwyk, Michael Schoenfeldt, Michael Sexton, William Sherman, Debora Shuger, James Siemon, James Simpson, Quentin Skinner, Emma Smith, Tiffany Stern, Richard Strier, Holger Schott Syme, Gordon Teskey, Ayanna Thompson, Stanley Wells, Benjamin Woodring, and David Wootton. All blunders in the book, of course, are entirely my responsibility.

Aubrey Everett has been a wonderfully gifted, thoughtful, and efficient assistant. The particularly lynx-eyed copy editor Don Rifkin at Norton made many valuable suggestions, as did Bailey Sincox. I have the opportunity once again to express my deep gratitude to Jill Kneerim, the best imaginable agent, and to Alane Mason, the best imaginable editor. I have already noted the role Ramie Targoff played in the instigation of this book. It remains only to express my love for her and for my wonderful, sustaining family.

NOTES

1. Citations of Buchanan are to George Buchanan, *A Dialogue on the Law of Kingship Among the Scots: A Critical Edition and Translation of George Buchanan's "De Iure Regni apud Scotos Dialogus,"* trans. Roger A. Mason and Martin S. Smith (Aldershot, U.K.: Ashgate, 2004).
2. According to the statute (Treasons Act, 26 Henry VIII, c. 13, in *Statutes of the Realm* 3.508), it was treason to "sclaunderously & malyciously publishe & pronounce, by expresse writinge or wordes, that the Kynge" was a schismatic, tyrant, infidel, or usurper of the Crown.
3. See Misha Teramura, "Richard Topcliffe's Informant: New Light on *The Isle of Dogs,*" in *Review of English Studies,* new series, 68 (2016), pp. 43–59. The loathsome Topcliffe was the government's most notorious interrogator, feared and hated for his sadism. The Catholic John Gerard, who was tortured by Topcliffe, characterized him as "the cruelest tyrant of all England" (46). In a splendid piece of detective work, Teramura identifies the chief informant, in the case of *The Isle of Dogs,* as the scoundrel William Udall.
4. All citations of Shakespeare are to *The Norton Shakespeare,* 3rd ed., ed. Stephen Greenblatt et al. (New York: W. W. Norton, 2016). About half of Shakespeare's plays exist in two versions with a claim to authority, a quarto and a folio. Except where noted, quotations derive from the First Folio text. (All versions are available on the digital site of *The Norton Shakespeare.*)
5. Derek Wilson, *Sir Francis Walsingham: A Courtier in an Age of Terror* (New York: Carroll and Graf, 2007), pp. 179–80.
6. "On the Religious Policies of the Queen (Letter to Critoy)." The letter was signed by Walsingham but was evidently prepared by Francis Bacon, in whose work it appears, in *Notes upon a Libel,* composed in 1592 but not published until 1861. The letter describes Elizabeth I as "not liking to make windows into men's hearts and secret

thoughts, except the abundance of them did overflow into overt and express acts or affirmations, tempered her law so as it straineth only manifest disobedience, in impugning and impeaching advisedly and maliciously her Majesty's supreme power, and maintaining and extolling a foreign jurisdiction." See Francis Bacon, *Early Writings: 1584–1596,* in *The Oxford Francis Bacon,* ed. Alan Stewart with Harriet Knight (Oxford: Clarendon, 2012) 1:35–36.

7. Cardinal of Como, letter of December 12, 1580, in Alison Plowden, *Danger to Elizabeth: The Catholics Under Elizabeth I* (New York: Stein and Day, 1973). Cf. Wilson, *Walsingham,* p. 105.

8. Wilson, *Walsingham,* p. 121.

9. F. G. Emmison, *Elizabethan Life: Disorder* (Chelmsford, U.K.: Essex County Council, 1970), pp. 57–58.

10. John Guy, *Elizabeth: The Forgotten Years* (New York: Viking, 2016), p. 364.

11. Playwrights could venture complimentary allusions to Elizabeth, as when Oberon, in *A Midsummer Night's Dream,* refers to the "imperial votress" whom Cupid's arrow missed. In Thomas Dekker's *Shoemakers' Holiday* (1600), the figure of the queen makes a cameo appearance.

12. In *How Shakespeare Put Politics on the Stage: Power and Succession in the History Plays* (New Haven and London: Yale University Press, 2016), the historian Peter Lake argues in rich detail that by the time he wrote *Henry V* Shakespeare had adopted "a distinctly Essexian agenda, organised around the national unity, and returning monarchical legitimacy, to be gained through a vigorous prosecution of war against a papalist, but by no means virulently popish, version of the foreign threat" (584). That this agenda proved to be a delusion and that Shakespeare therefore got it all wrong only proves, Lake concludes, "that it is not necessary to be politically correct, or at least correct about politics, to write plays that last" (603).

13. Essex's insult is reported by Sir Walter Ralegh in his posthumously published *The Prerogative of Parlaments* [sic] *in England* (London, 1628), p. 43. In Ralegh's view, Essex's intemperate words "cost him his head, which his insurrection had not cost him, but for that speech."

14. Guy, *Elizabeth,* 339.

15. In the government-authorized *Declaration of the Practises and Treasons . . . by Robert Late Earle of Essex,* Francis Bacon suggested that Meyrick wanted to see enacted in the theater what he hoped Essex

would accomplish in reality: "So earnest hee was to satisfie his eyes with the sight of that tragedie which hee thought soon after his lord should bring from the stage to the state" (quoted in E. K. Chambers, *William Shakespeare: A Study of Facts and Problems*, 2 vols. [Oxford: Clarendon, 1930], 2:326).

16. By the statute of 25 Edward III, c. 2, it was an act of treason: When a Man doth compass or imagine the Death of our Lord the King, or of our Lady his [Queen] or of their eldest Son and Heir; or if a Man do violate the King's [Companion,] or the King's eldest daughter unmarried, or the Wife [of] the King's eldest Son and Heir; or if a Man do levy War against our Lord the King in his Realm, or be adherent to the King's Enemies in his Realm, giving to them Aid and Comfort in the Realm, or elsewhere (*Statutes of the Realm*, 1.319–20; brackets are per the original).

I am indebted to ongoing work on this subject by Nicholas Utzig.

17. See Jason Scott-Warren, "Was Elizabeth I Richard II? The Authenticity of Lambarde's 'Conversation,'" *Review of English Studies* 64 (2012), pp. 208–30.

18. Manningham (1602) in Chambers, *William Shakespeare*, 2:212.

19. In *Narrative and Dramatic Sources of Shakespeare*, ed. Geoffrey Bullough, 8 vols. (New York: Columbia University Press, 1977), 5:557. See, likewise, *The Arden Shakespeare: Coriolanus*, ed. Peter Holland (London: Bloomsbury, 2013), pp. 60–61.

20. On the affinities between Shakespeare and modern mass entertainment, see Jeffrey Knapp, *Pleasing Everyone: Mass Entertainment in Renaissance London and Golden-Age Hollywood* (Oxford: Oxford University Press, 2017).

21. Ben Jonson, *Bartholomew Fair*, ed. Eugene M. Waith (New Haven: Yale University Press, 1963), Induction, lines 78–80.

INDEX